ANSWERS TO COMMON QUESTIONS ABOUT

God

Titles in the Answers to Common Questions Series

Answers to Common Questions About Angels & Demons
by H. Wayne House and Timothy J. Demy

Answers to Common Questions About God
by H. Wayne House and Timothy J. Demy

Answers to Common Questions About Heaven & Eternity
by Timothy J. Demy and Thomas Ice

Answers to Common Questions About Jesus
by H. Wayne House and Timothy J. Demy

Answers to Common Questions About the Bible
by H. Wayne House and Timothy J. Demy

Answers to Common Questions About the End Times
by Timothy J. Demy and Thomas Ice

ANSWERS TO COMMON QUESTIONS ABOUT

God

H. Wayne House
Timothy J. Demy

Kregel
Publications

Printed in the United States of America

13 14 15 16 17 / 5 4 3 2 1

To the memory of Carl F. H. Henry,
scholar, teacher, mentor, friend

Contents

About This Series 11
Introduction 13

Part 1: Initial Questions About God 15
1. How do we know that God exists? *15*
2. How are we able to know about God? *26*
3. In what sense is God knowable and unknowable? *28*
4. Where did God come from, if anywhere? (Aseity) *29*
5. Is human language truly capable of talking about God? *30*
6. What do we mean when we speak of God as a personal being? *33*

Part 2: The Attributes of God 35
7. How do we categorize the attributes of God? *35*
8. In what ways is God like us and not like us? *40*
9. Has God always existed? (Eternity) *44*
10. Does God know everything? (Omniscience) *46*
11. Is God all-powerful? (Omnipotence) *47*
12. Is God everywhere? (Omnipresence) *49*
13. Does God ever change? (Immutability) *51*
14. What does it mean that God is holy? *53*
15. What is meant by God's goodness? *54*
16. What does it mean that God is sovereign? *56*
17. What is the veracity of God? *58*

18. What does it mean that God is love? *60*
19. Does God feel our pain? *61*
20. Is God all-wise? *62*
21. What do we mean when we say that God is one?
    (Simple being) *64*
22. What is meant by God's spirituality? *65*
23. What does it mean for God to be longsuffering? *68*
24. What is God's mercy? *70*
25. What is God's grace? *71*
26. What about the problem of God and evil? *71*

Part 3: The Names of God   75
27. What is the proper name of God? *75*
28. What does Scripture mean by the name of God in
    the singular? *79*
29. Is the name Father ever applied to God in the
    Old Testament? *80*
30. Is the name Son ever applied to God in the
    Old Testament? *82*
31. Is the name Holy Spirit ever applied to God in the
    Old Testament? *82*
32. What is the meaning of the name *Elohim*? *84*
33. What is the meaning of the names *El* and *Eloah*? *86*
34. What is the meaning of *El Shaddai*? *88*
35. What is the meaning *Adonai*? *88*
36. In what sense is God known as *Baal*? *88*
37. Are Father, Son, and Holy Spirit names of God
    in the New Testament? *89*

**Part 4: The Trinity and Intrapersonal Relationship
of God   91**
38. In what sense is God both one and three? *91*
39. How do the three persons share the same nature? *93*
40. Is the Son in subordination to the Father? *94*

41. What is the difference between the ontological Trinity and the economic Trinity? *96*

Part 5: Early Heresies Relating to God and How the Church Responded to Them 98

42. What is the heresy of modalism and what was the church's response? (Modalistic monarchianism) *98*
43. What is the heresy of Arianism and what was the church's response? *100*
44. What is the heresy of unitarianism? (Dynamic monarchianism) *104*
45. What is the heresy of open theism? *105*

Part 6: What the Ancient Church Taught About God 111

46. What is the Apostles' Creed? *111*
47. What is the Nicene Creed? *113*
48. What is the Constantinopolitan Creed? *114*
49. What is the Council of Ephesus? (Mother of God) *117*
50. What is the Chalcedonian Creed? *118*
51. What is the Athanasian Creed? *119*

Part 7: The True and Living God and Other Gods 121

52. How is the God of the Bible distinguished from other deities? *121*
53. Do all religions lead to God? *122*
54. What does God say about other religions? *125*
55. Does a person's belief about God affect how he or she lives? *126*

Conclusion 127
Notes 129
Recommended Reading 145
About the Authors 149

About This Series

The Answers to Common Questions series is designed to provide readers a brief summary and overview of individual topics and issues in Christian theology. For quick reference and ease in studying, the works are written in a question and answer format. The questions follow a logical progression so that those reading straight through a work will receive a greater appreciation for the topic and the issues involved. The volumes are thorough, though not exhaustive, and can be used as a set or as single-volume studies. Each volume is fully documented and contains a recommended reading list for those who want to pursue the subject in greater detail.

The study of theology and the many issues within Christianity is an exciting and rewarding endeavor. For two thousand years, Christians have proclaimed the gospel of Jesus Christ and sought to accurately define and defend the doctrines of their faith as recorded in the Bible. In 2 Timothy 2:15, Christians are exhorted: "Be diligent to present yourself approved to God as a workman who does not need to be ashamed, accurately handling the word of truth." The goal of these books is to help you in your diligence and accuracy as you study God's Word and its influence in history and thought through the centuries.

Introduction

I [we] believe in one God, the Father, the Almighty, maker of heaven and earth, of all that is, seen and unseen." So begins the Nicene Creed (known more technically as the Nicene-Constantinopolitan Creed), dating back to the fourth century and recited daily by millions of Christians around the world for more than 1,600 years. The first words of the creed can be summarized in one word: *monotheism*. At the core of Christianity lies belief in one God. This does not deny the existence of the Trinity—God the Father, God the Son, and God the Holy Spirit. That too is a central teaching of orthodox Christianity and will be considered in part in the following pages. However, in these pages it is primarily the person and work of God the Father that we will consider.

Everyone has conceptions (and misconceptions) about God. For some, God is like a divine Teddy Bear; for others, God is a raging monster. For some, God is a personal being who is intimately concerned with every detail in the lives of humans; for others, God is an apathetic, impersonal entity who may as well be dying or dead. Throughout the centuries, Christians have affirmed the biblical teaching that God is a personal being who establishes relationships with individuals created in His image.

God has told us about Himself through general revelation in nature and through specific revelation in the Bible. Those are the only ways we can know about God. "Apart from God's initiative,

God's act, God's revelation, no confident basis exists for God-talk."[1]
Fortunately we have such revelation. Join us as we take a look at the
pages of Scripture to see what it tells us about God.

PART 1

Initial Questions About God

1. How do we know that God exists?[1]

The Bible's first verse begins with the assumption that God exists and that He is the creator of the universe. But can we simply make such an assumption? Don't we first need to be able to prove His existence?

Actually, before we can move to the question of God's existence, we must ask some prior questions. First, what do we mean by the question "Does God exist?" One person may be questioning whether an actual being exists, while another may only be asking whether a concept of God is in view and a valid presupposition. For Christians, the issue is whether the God presented in the Bible exists. The Bible is not concerned to prove that some kind of god exists, but to explain what kind of God exists and how to know this God.

Christian theology is mainly interested in understanding the God who has chosen to reveal Himself to us, especially in the Bible. Arguments for God's existence, though interesting and helpful, are not essential to our experience with God. Such arguments, rational in their nature, can only point to the probability, however high, for the existence of a powerful and intelligent higher being. They cannot describe the fullness of the biblical God's nature.

Nevertheless, the arguments for God's existence can reinforce our Christian belief, removing obstacles to faith, and can cause an unbeliever to examine evidence for the Christian God.

There are a number of classic arguments for the existence of God, but we will only deal with three of them: the *cosmological*, the *teleological*, and the *anthropological* (or moral) arguments.

Cosmological Argument

The cosmological argument addresses the question of cause. What caused the creation of the world? There are only three options, two of which are impossible. After they are excluded, only one remains: that a creator created the universe.

The first option is that the universe created itself. Some prominent scientists hold this view today. But self-creation is contrary to the law of non-contradiction: "Two opposites cannot both be true in the same way at the same time." For the universe to be uncreated and yet be able to create would require it to simultaneously be and yet not be.

Another cosmological explanation is that time and chance brought the universe into existence. According to the old cliché, given enough time and chance, anything can happen. This is manifestly false. Even given trillions of years and billions of chances—far more than postulated by people who advocate this perspective—chance and time cannot cause creation because chance and time have no causative capacity to create. Chance is not a thing but a mathematical abstraction, and time is a measurement of motion and change and not a causative thing in itself. Because neither chance nor time is an agent or cause of anything, they cannot create.

Both of these supposed explanations are absurd, like a two-angled triangle or a square circle. By definition, these things are self-contradictions. In the same way, a violation of the law of non-contradiction poses an absurdity. Nothing cannot produce something.

Stephen Hawking, in his book *The Grand Design*, argues that the beginning of the universe was inevitable because of the law of gravity. He writes, "Because there is a law like gravity, the universe can and will create itself from nothing,"[2] and, "Spontaneous creation is the reason there is something rather than nothing, why the universe exists, why we exist."[3] He writes as a former professor of mathematics at Cambridge, occupying the Lucasian Chair, a position that Sir Isaac Newton occupied. Newton believed that the universe could not arise from chaos but demanded a creator.[4] Hawking, conversely, believes that a theoretical law of how things would work if they existed can somehow bring into existence the things it would govern.

But simply having a theory of something does not mean that the something must exist. For example, if we were to describe how a unicorn would look if it existed, this does not mean that unicorns therefore exist or that describing one can produce one. Only the mind of an infinite, personal being who existed prior to creation can bring into existence something out of nothing (*creation ex nihilo*).[5]

Hawking believes that the first objection to Newton's view occurred in 1992, when a planet was observed orbiting a star outside of our solar system. He says, "That makes the coincidences of our planetary conditions—the single sun, the lucky combination of Earth-sun distance and solar mass—far less remarkable, and far less compelling as evidence that the Earth was carefully designed just to please us human beings."[6]

But such an observation in no way disproves that a creator created the universe, nor does it demonstrate that the earth was not carefully designed "just to please us human beings." The Creator looked at the universe He had created and declared it good (Gen. 1:4, 10, 18, 21, 25) before humans had ever been created, not merely after it had been made useable by humans. He pronounced it *very good* (Gen. 1:31) *after* the creation of the humans for whom He made it.

The fine-tuning of our earth and universe represents the exactitude of an infinite mind who desires order in the universe and solar system He created.[7] This is the assertion of the anthropic principle. This philosophical perspective maintains that the universe appears designed to support the life of those who observe its design. But God's purpose in engineering it this way was not simply to please humans; it was to accomplish what was necessary to ensure the furtherance of humanity for His own purposes.[8]

Though Hawking says that "philosophy is dead,"[9] Plato is much alive. Even Hawking's views are belied in his book as he grapples with ideas that cannot be physically demonstrated; thus, even if he rebels against the mind, he must use the mind to make his arguments.

What about Hawking's insistence that Newton has been overturned because a planet exists outside our solar system, unconnected to humanity? Hawking incorrectly insinuates that everything the Creator creates must be prepared for human life. But the planets and sun of this solar system, as well as those of other systems, may serve for exploration by humanity (even though such exploration is limited when contrasted with the vastness of the universe), which pleases God, and not merely to please humans. The Creator delights in His creation.

Thomas Aquinas (1225–1274), a major architect of the cosmological argument, rightly argued that every effect has a cause. Not every thing must have a cause but every effect must have a cause.

The Law of Causality[10]

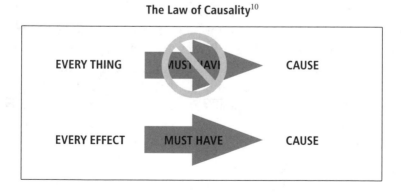

Consequently, there must be a first cause because there cannot be an infinite regress of finite causes. This principle only says that every *effect* must have a cause, not that every *thing* must have a cause. There is a necessary first cause, an uncaused cause. We call this cause God.

Mathematician and philosopher Gottfried Wilhelm Leibniz posed the problem, "Why is there something rather than nothing?"[11] One may find the answer only by looking at the something that lies beyond the nothing. In addition, as Ludwig Wittgenstein stated, "Solving the solution of the riddle of life in space and time lies *outside* space and time."[12] Hawking, and others are looking at the universe when the answer lies outside the universe.

Teleology

A second support for the existence of God resides in the subject of design, or *teleology*, from the Greek word *telos* for purpose or goal. Teleological arguments for the existence of God are based on the observation of order and/or design in the universe. Such arguments argue that order is obvious in the universe; therefore there must be an "orderer."

Theologian Thomas Oden says, "The power of this argument is best seen by taking seriously its opposite hypothesis, that there is no cause of order. For then one is attributing the order to chance, which in the long run still would leave the order unexplained."[13] Since this observable order cannot be attributed to the object itself, the observable order argues for an intelligent being who has established the order. This being is God.

Listen to the words of theologian and physicist Stanley L. Jaki: "[The universe] has supreme coherence from the very small to the very large. It is a consistent unity free of debilitating paradoxes. It is beautifully proportioned into layers or dimensions and yet all of them are in perfect interaction."[14]

The design argument contends that non-conscious things have a purpose which cannot be the result of impersonal cause. Intelligent-design scientists attempt to demonstrate that the universe and life show signs of a designer through two primary ways: the studies of *specified complexity* and *irreducible complexity*.

Specified Complexity

A string of letters provides a good example of specified complexity. While some sequences of letters may form a recognizable pattern or provide information, that does not mean the sequences were designed. Moreover, just because something is complex does not make it designed. What is necessary is for both specificity and complexity to be present.

The ARN website supplies a helpful explanation of specified complexity: "When a design theorist says that a string of letters is *specified*, he's saying that it fits a recognizable pattern. When he says it is complex, he is saying there are so many different ways the object could have turned out that the chance of getting any particular outcome by accident is hopelessly small."[15]

Derived from a combination of four letters that could have been randomly formed, the word *blue* does provide information, a recognizable pattern, but it is not complex. Conversely, a lengthy combination of letters, as seen in the chart below, clearly is complex, but it provides no information. But when something demonstrates a recognizable pattern *and* is complex, we can be sure it has been designed.

Specified Complexity Demonstrates Intelligent Design[16]

Specification Does *Not* Demonstrate Intelligent Design
BLUE
Complexity Does *Not* Demonstrate Intelligent Design
ZOEFFNPBINNGQZAMZQPEGOXSYFMRTEXRNYGRRGN NFVGUMLMTYQTXTXWORNBWIGBBCVHPUZMWLON HATQUGOTFJKZXFHP
Specified Complexity *Does* Demonstrate Intelligent Design
FOURSCOREANDSEVENYEARSAGOOURFATHERSBROU GHTFORTHONTHISCONTINENTANEWNATIONCONCEI VEDINLIBERTY

In the chart above, only the last example possesses both specificity and complexity, clearly demonstrating an intelligence behind the formulation. Such a complex informational statement could not have happened by accident.

Irreducible Complexity

Irreducible complexity can be described like this: If a biological system (or "machine") has interdependent components that are necessary to its operation, without which it would cease to function, then it could not have evolved.[17] Biochemist Michael Behe has been at the forefront of this view. He has identified a number of systems that had to have existed in composition from the start or else they would not be functional. Behe is simply responding to the challenge of Charles Darwin, who said, "If it could be demonstrated that any complex organ existed which could not possibly have been formed by numerous, successive slight modifications, my theory would absolutely break down."[18]

Behe has used the mousetrap and the flagellum as examples. The first is an inanimate machine; the second, a biological system. In order for there to be a mousetrap, certain parts must work in concert and exist simultaneously, namely, the base, the hammer, the spring, the hold-down bar, and the catch. If any of these is missing, the mousetrap will not work to catch mice. In his book, *Only a Theory*, Kenneth R. Miller recounts an experiment of one of his classmates, who

> struck upon the brilliant idea of using an old, broken mousetrap as a spitball catapult, and it worked brilliantly. . . . It had worked perfectly as something other than a mousetrap. . . . my rowdy friend had pulled a couple of parts . . . probably the hold-down bar and catch—off the trip to make it easier to conceal and more effective as a catapult. . . . [leaving] the base, the spring, and the hammer. Not

much of a mousetrap. . . . I realized why [Behe's] mousetrap analogy had bothered me. It was wrong. The mousetrap is not irreducibly complex after all.[19]

In reality, Miller's friend had not created a mousetrap at all, and so had not disproved Behe's illustration. Once several components were removed—by intelligence and not by accident, incidentally—the result was no longer a mousetrap. It was a catapult. The fact that it borrowed some of the common elements of the mousetrap (in the same way that biological machines have some of the same components as other biological systems) does not turn a catapult into a mousetrap.

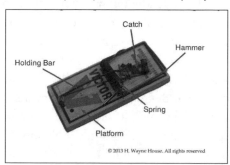

Mousetrap Example of Irreducible Complexity

Catch

Hammer

Holding Bar

Spring

Platform

When looking at the nature of a thing, its being, it is not only the similarities that define it but also the dissimilarities. In the case at hand, similar components formed a different reality, but the way in which those components were put together and functioned together was dissimilar. That various mechanical and biological machines have similar parts does not prove that they are mechanically or organically related, but that they are framed on a common design.

Darwin understood the absolute imperative of incremental changes in living organisms for his theory to work, but unfortunately, many of his disciples cling needlessly to his flawed theory. That theory may explain variation among species and sometimes genus, but not a vertical move from lower forms of life to more advanced living organisms.

Darwin's Words on What Would Disprove His Theory[20]

"If it could be demonstrated that any complex organ existed which could not possibly have been formed by numerous, successive slight modifications, my theory would absolutely break down."

Charles Darwin,
The Origin of Species: A Facsimile of the First Edition, p. 189

Moral Argument

The moral argument for the existence of God is based on the concept of conscience. The Darwinian evolutionary perspective has difficulty explaining moral conscience or impulse since it is contrary to the survival of the fittest and would not develop as an aspect of natural selection.

Everyone has a moral impulse—a categorical imperative, to use Immanuel Kant's expression. According to Kant, since moral decisions are not necessarily rewarded in this life, there must be a basis for moral actions that are beyond this life. This implies the ideas of immortality and ultimate judgment, as well as a God who establishes and demands morality. He does this by rewarding good and punishing evil.

Those who reject the idea of absolute moral causes subscribe to a self-refuting argument (for example, to say there are no absolutes is an absolute statement). Moreover, such a notion leads logically to the inability to distinguish between a Mother Teresa and an Adolf Hitler. In the words of C. S. Lewis, "If no set of moral ideas were truer or better than any other, there would be no sense in preferring civilised morality to savage morality, or Christian morality to Nazi morality."[21]

How does all of this relate to proving the existence of God?

Hasting Rashdall: "A moral ideal can exist nowhere and nohow but in a Mind; an absolute moral ideal can exist only in a Mind from which all Reality is derived. Our moral ideal can only claim objective validity in so far as it can rationally be regarded as the revelation of a moral ideal eternally existing in the mind of God."[22]

Self-Refuting (Moral) Argument

The classical approach to the moral argument is similar to that of the cosmological argument. Within everyone is an awareness of "oughtness." Where does it come from? It could not come from nothing, so it must have a source. Kant's idea of oughtness can be described as follows:

1. The greatest good of all persons is to do what is right, an unconditional duty.
2. All persons should strive for the greatest good.
3. Whatever persons ought to do, they are able to do.
4. However, persons are unable to realize the greatest good in this life without God.
5. Therefore we must posit both a future life and God.[23]

C. S. Lewis maintained that without a universal moral law, (1) moral disagreements would make no sense; (2) all moral criticisms would be meaningless; (3) it would be unnecessary to keep promises or treaties; and (4) we would not make excuses for breaking a moral law.[24] Lewis says that such a universal moral law requires a universal Moral Law Giver, since the source of the law provides moral commandments and is interested in human behavior. This Moral Law Giver must be absolutely good; otherwise, all moral effort would be futile since we would be dedicating and even sacrificing our lives for what is not ultimately moral. Moreover, the standard of all good must be completely good. Consequently, there must be an absolutely good Moral Law Giver.

Another part of the moral argument, conceived by Blaise Pascal and known as the Wager Argument for God's existence, is based on the concept of *risk*. As the argument illustrates, one makes a risk based on gain versus loss. At life's end, a Christian, if correct, gains heaven; the non-Christian, if correct, simply ceases to exist. If the Christian is wrong, he or she will become nonexistent. But the non-Christian, if wrong, will incur hell.

The first part of the Wager Argument cannot be avoided. Pascal continues that if God does not exist, the believer has nothing to lose; that person is still able to live a good life. The Christian has no possibility of being disappointed nor the non-Christian of being rewarded. If the Christian is wrong, he or she will never know it. But if the unbeliever is right, he will never have the pleasure of knowing it; however, if he is wrong, he will know it for eternity.

In the words of Pascal, "I will tell you that you will thereby gain in this life, and that, at each step you take on this road, you will see so great certainty of gain, so much nothingness in what you risk, that you will at last recognise that you have wagered for something certain and infinite, for which you have given nothing."[25]

What Do the Arguments for God's Existence Prove?

These arguments may encourage the believer and function as testimonies or aids in pondering the massive truth of God's existence. Norman Geisler and Paul Feinberg sum it up well: "Faith in

God is not based on evidence but on the authority of God Himself through His revelation. . . . Even though one cannot reason to belief in God, he can find reasons for it. In fact faith may be defined as 'the ability to reason with assent'"[26]

2. How are we able to know about God?

God has chosen to reveal Himself to humanity in two ways: first, in nature; and second, through special revelation. *Natural revelation* is given by God to all and intended for all, whereas *special revelation* is given to a few but also intended for all. Natural revelation declares God's greatness. Special revelation declares God's grace.

Natural Revelation

God has revealed Himself in several interactions with humanity. The natural world around us shows His glory. According to Psalm 19:1, "The heavens declare the glory of God, and the sky proclaims the work of His hands" (HCSB). The psalm continues with a description of the revelation of God in nature. Daily He reveals Himself without speaking audible words. The message goes throughout the world. The physical expression of God's revelation may be seen in the Sun's course across the skies from one end of the earth to the other.

But God has not only made Himself known in the larger working of the solar system and the universe. He also reveals Himself through the beauty and wonder of nature in its order and design, and also in the way that He cares for us. The words of Jesus say as much: God brings the rain on the just and unjust alike (Matt 5:45).

Another way in which God has made Himself known is by His imprint on human moral consciousness. As was argued in question one regarding the existence of God, our moral nature arises from God's moral nature. This is another way in which we learn about God, in that we are similar to Him in some respects.

Lastly, within each of us is an innate religious impulse. St. Augustine said, "You encourage [humans] to delight to praise you, for you have made us for yourself, and our heart is restless until it rests in you."[27] Humans are incurably religious, a fact borne out by the existence of religions from the beginning of mankind's existence. While this religious yearning displays many forms, nonetheless it testifies to an inward call from God in nature. Even atheists profess their belief in a religious manner; they still seek for ultimate purpose in the world.

Unfortunately, as Paul tells us in Roman 1:18–32, this religious impulse does not lead people to the true God but to idolatry. God must reveal Himself in a special manner, through the work of the gospel and the Holy Spirit in the heart of the unbeliever, if a person is to be saved.

Special Revelation

God has not only spoken in nature but also by special revelation, in which the Creator-Savior enters in among humanity to do a special act of grace. God's revelation is intended for all people but is received only by some. Whereas natural revelation is sufficient for condemnation, special revelation is sufficient for salvation. Natural revelation declares God's greatness, but special revelation declares God's grace.

The author of Hebrews begins his book as follows: "Long ago God spoke to the fathers by the prophets at different times and in different ways. In these last days, He has spoken to us by His Son" (Heb. 1:1–2 HCSB). The Creator of all has demonstrated His character throughout His historical interaction with mankind. From the time that He walked and talked with Adam and Eve, to His subsequent revelation to Noah, the patriarchs, Moses, and Israel, He has shown Himself to be an infinite yet personal Deity through His words and works. He gave a promise to our first parents in Genesis 3:15, one of final victory over sin. He rescued a family from the flood after every thought of sinful mankind had become evil. He came to Abraham with a promise that through him, God would brings blessing to the entire earth. Finally, He came in human form and nature to offer Himself and fulfill His commitment to His people and all mankind.

We may know God, but only in the way He desires and according to the timing He established in eternity. By responding to His revelation, we can come to truth and salvation. As the apostle John said, "This is eternal life: that they may know You, the only true God, and the One You have sent—Jesus Christ" (John 17:3 HCSB).

3. In what sense is God knowable and unknowable?

The God of the universe cannot be known through human effort. Only by His own effort to communicate with His creation can He be seen in earthly terms. At least four millennia ago, a friend of Job's named Zophar spoke these words:

> Can you fathom the depths of God
> or discover the limits of the Almighty?
> They are higher than the heavens—what can you do?
> They are deeper than Sheol—what can you know?
> Their measure is longer than the earth
> and wider than the sea.   (Job 11:7–9 HCSB)

Note that this passage does not say God cannot be known, only that a human being cannot penetrate the infinite Deity. Being finite, each of us has limited abilities to learn about God. We can know Him only to the degree that He reveals Himself to us. Moreover, were He to reveal a great amount of His infinite being, our finite minds could not contain the truth.

The apostle Paul says in Romans 1:18–24 that God is both knowable and known by people, for aspects of His divine being—His eternal power and divine nature—have been clearly seen since the creation of the world. Consequently, people are without excuse. The apostle continues, "For though they knew God, they did not glorify Him as God or show gratitude" (v. 21 HCSB). The result of what people know about God does not bring gratitude to God for all He has done, but rejection of the revelation and the replacement of this knowledge with foolishness, even of worshipping the creation and not the Creator.

Only those who by faith fully embrace God can truly (though not fully) know Him or rightly appreciate His general revelation in nature. Jesus said that He is the way, the truth, and the life, and that no person can come to the Father except through the Son. To know the Son is to know the Father (John 14:6–7).

The apostle Paul puts all of this into perspective as we finite beings praise a God whom we can only know through His own self-revelation:

> Oh, the depth of the riches
> both of the wisdom and the knowledge of God!
> How unsearchable His judgments
> and untraceable His ways!
> For who has known the mind of the Lord?
> Or who has been His counselor?
> Or who has ever first given to Him,
> and has to be repaid?
> For from Him and through Him
> and to Him are all things.
> To Him be the glory forever. Amen.
>   (Rom. 11:33–36 HCSB)

4. Where did God come from, if anywhere? (Aseity)

One of the early questions of many children is, "Where did God come from?" It is a natural question. Everything we know of—a car, ice cream, a Christmas toy, even a baby brother—has a beginning. When we considered arguments for the existence of God, we learned that every effect has a cause. But there is one uncaused cause: God.

So the answer to the above question is, "God came from no-where," or, "There never was a time when God was not."

In theology, we use the term *aseity*, meaning that the source of God's existence is wholly within Himself. This is a hard concept to grasp since every other thing in our experience is contrary to it. There is no possibility that there is an infinite regress of matter that never had a beginning under any laws known to humans. All matter had a beginning. But an infinite, non-material, non-temporal, and non-spatial being has no such restrictions, and His uncreated existence violates none of the basic laws of logic. A God who has always been is the most likely source of everything that is not Himself.

5. Is human language truly capable of talking about God?

Try to describe anything to anyone without using words. It's impossible. Words are the means by which we form and communicate ideas. It should be no surprise, then, that language about God is a necessary part of acquiring our knowledge about God. Some claim to know Him through mystical experience, and there is no doubt that believers have a spiritual experience with God. But whenever we speak about truth, knowledge, faith (which is legitimate only when based on fact), and consequently, God, we depend on language.

The word *God* means something to us. Those who hold to a realist theology believe the word refers to something or someone real. Others may refer to God as a means to speak of human existence, whether or not the theological language even refers to an existing God, somewhat like speaking of elves or Santa Claus.

Some world religions, such as Buddhism, speak of God as an abstract, impersonal being or concept. Others, such as Hinduism, see God as a generalized term that includes multiple deities—representations or manifestations of the One. Still others view God in terms of orthodox Christianity, as a personal, infinite being.

The Bible is a book of words about God and from God. Apart

from words, it is hard to imagine that we can know God, for He has always revealed Himself through language. Beginning with the garden of Eden, God *spoke*—first to Adam and Eve, then on throughout the unfolding history of His revelation to humanity.

Yet in describing the being and acts of God, we encounter the limitations of human language. We are attempting to associate known words, concepts, and images with the unknown. God is an infinite being, beyond time and space, and is not identified with His creation. There is no one like Him, and what we know of Him is limited by what He has revealed as well as our capacity to understand much that is above our comprehension. When we speak of Him, we can do so only imperfectly.

There are three ways in which we may speak about divine reality: *equivocal, univocal,* and *analogical.*

To describe something equivocally means that we ascribe a specific meaning to a term that could have other meanings, all depending on how it is used. How we understand an equivocal term depends on its context. For example, a person might use the word *buck* to refer to a dollar in currency. But in another context, buck would refer to a male deer. If someone says, "I killed a buck," the meaning could be confusing without a proper context. Does the speaker mean he spent a dollar or shot a deer? Again, when someone says "pitcher," is he speaking of an object that can hold a liquid or of someone who throws a baseball over home plate?

Using the word wrongly in a particular context would be called equivocation. In reference to God, since we are using finite language, it sometimes becomes necessary to explain the unexplainable by speaking in the negative, that is, what is not God. Hopefully what God is not will give some sense of what God is.

A second form of language is called univocal, related to the word *univocation.* Something is univocal if it has only one possible meaning. Something is univocal if it would have the same meaning regardless of its context, making it hard to be misunderstood. For example, if a teacher asks a boy to put his finger on his nose, the meaning is clear. The statements, "The building is tall," and, "The man is tall," are both univocal. How tall they are is irrelevant; the only concern is the quality of tallness.

Someone who believes we can speak of God univocally believes that in saying "God is good" or "John is good," we mean essentially the same thing. But this is unlikely. Similarly, to say that a woman has an arm is not the same thing as saying that God has an arm. In univocal use of language, there is unity between the word and what it represents. But this does not apply when using finite meanings to describe an infinite being.

The last perspective, analogical, is a middle position between univocal and equivocal language. It is actually a combination of the two. If a woman says she is going to be toast when she gets home because she stayed too long at work, we would understand that she is in trouble when she arrives home. The guest of honor at a celebrity roast isn't going to be burned at the stake; he is simply going to have harmless jokes told about him. There are both similarities and differences in meaning between an athlete running a hundred-yard race on the track and a train running on the track.

We generally use analogical speech in making statements about God's being and actions. Words and concepts share similar meanings in the finite world as they do when speaking of the infinite being, but their similarity is by analogy rather than equality. The goodness of God is like the goodness of a human, but they are not equal to each other.[28] Since nothing in creation truly describes the God who exists apart and before creation, our descriptions of Him can only approximate Him. When the Scripture speaks of God's emotions or mental state with ideas like God repenting or forgetting, it speaks not of the actual acts of God but of how He is perceived. When the text says something about God's eyes or arm, it does not mean that God has physical organs or appendages; rather, it is describing how God acts within the created order by using terms we can relate to through our own acts within the created order.

In summary, viewing God in equivocal terms gives evangelical scholars little way to truly understand Him. Some evangelical theologians do understand God univocally, believing that the way in which we speak of God is the same sense that God means. But most evangelicals accept that the biblical text and our language speak of God analogically. We do not have the capacity to express God in His perfection and infinite nature. But we do have concepts, and even feelings, that are similar to what God Himself speaks.

Types of Language That May Be Used to Speak About God[29]

Equivocal	Univocal	Analogical
Term employed in only one sense, so a term has completely different meanings in a context from its other meanings.	Term employed predicatively with different subjects has the same meaning in both instances.	This is a combination of equivocal and univocal sense.
A *row* of trees and *row* the boat.	The man is *tall* and the building is *tall*.	Jeff *runs* the 100-yard dash, and the train *runs* down the track.

6. What do we mean when we speak of God as a personal being?

It is important to understand what it means for God to be a person (in contrast with His divine nature). God's personhood is not the same as human personhood. In a human person, the person and his nature are one. But God is three persons who share all of the same attributes, including the same intellect and will.

The first chapter of Genesis states that God created humans in the image of God (Gen. 1:26), and humans are the only creatures to have been created like this. We are created to resemble God (though obviously not exactly). He made us personal beings, even as He is personal. Because of his personal nature, He can relate to us personally. This is different from the religious perspective of pantheism and true of much Eastern thought and some scientists' view of God, in which God is no more than an abstraction. Because we are created in God's image, He is no less personal than we are.

Though theologians commonly speak of anthropomorphisms and anthropopathisms in referring to God—meaning that we speak of God in human terms regarding figures of speech in the Bible—it is often not acknowledged that we humans are theomorphic (shaped like God). This distinction became part of the author's understanding of God and human nature several decades ago and seems a better way to think of God and us in His image. We are created in the image of God, not only spiritually but also physically. By this, we are not advocating that God is physical; rather, we mean that God created humans not only as spiritual beings, but also as physical beings to reflect what God is without a physical body. As the author (Wayne) has said elsewhere,

> Remember, humans were created in the image of God, so we are *theomorphic*—that is, after the form of God. He has created us with abilities or attributes that approximate in part what He is apart from finitude and from human form. God sees and we see, but we do so with the physical organs while God sees in infinity without physical eyes. We think and God thinks, but we do so in a limited manner and sequentially, while God thinks infinitely and intuitively with all knowledge being instantly before Him.[30]

Because God acts, thinks, wills, relates, and emotes, He has created us to do the same as finite beings. We act personally, because God is a person, but we do not act perfectly or in an infinite way.

PART 2

The Attributes of God

7. How do we categorize the attributes of God?

Initial Considerations

An infinite Deity is difficult to understand and explain. Finite humans can only understand Him in a finite way. Only this infinite God can fully understand Himself and His creation, and He is able to do so because ultimate truth dwells in Him.

Knowledge of God, whether by Himself or by us, is based on the laws of logic. Even God cannot be other than what is consistent with His own nature. To argue that God is illogical and yet attempt to make a statement about God's being is to "indulge in religious babbling," according to Carl F. H. Henry.[1]

The Incomparability of Yahweh

The Creator of the universe is unique. There are many so-called gods but only one true and living God. Though false deities may be ascribed certain attributes similar to those of the God of the Bible, those deities are neither true nor living. Not only are the gods depicted in stone or metal idols false, but gods of the mind are equally false.

The biblical text sets forth a Divine Being who cannot be truly compared with the gods of the nations, and this is presented in three ways.[2] First is the negative expression, "there is none like," as found in 1 Samuel:

> There is no one holy like Yahweh,
> Indeed, there is no one besides You,
> Nor is there any rock like our God.
> (1 Sam. 2:2; see also Exod. 9:14;
> Ps. 86:8; Jer. 10:6–7)

Second, the biblical authors ask the question, "Who is like?" as found in Psalm 113:5: "Who is like Yahweh our God, Who is enthroned on high?" (see also Jer. 49:19; Isa. 44:7; Exod. 15:11; Mic. 7:18).

The third kind of passage on God's incomparability is the inclusion of verbs that signify equality and similarity. An example may be found in Psalm 89:6 (NKJV): "For who in the heavens can be compared to Yahweh? Who among the sons of the mighty can be likened to Yahweh?" (See also Ps. 40:5; Isa. 40:25.)

God is unique, and this uniqueness relates to His incomparable nature. He is the only One to be worshipped, who can give eternal life and can forgive sins.[3]

The Use of the Term Attribute

The word *attribute* refers to the inherent qualities or properties that make something what it is. A. H. Strong says, "The attributes of God are those distinguishing characteristics of the divine nature which are inseparable from the idea of God and which constitute the basis and ground for his various manifestations to his creatures."[4] W. Robert Cook explains an attribute as "an essential or property which is intrinsic to its subject. It is that by which it may be distinguished or identified."[5]

The Relation Between the Essence and Attributes of God

Since the infinite Deity exists outside of space and time and is a simple being rather than complex one, He is not to be understood as having parts that are divided in His being. He is not all-powerful as opposed to all-just, or transcendent as opposed to immanent. Humans, however, have difficulty in speaking of God and His actions in the world without addressing His attributes separately. Human nature allows us to express our own attributes in contradictory ways, for we are often fickle. But God is consistent and uniform in His attributes, so that they all work in absolute, unwavering concert and unity.

Consequently, the oneness of God's properties may be said to be His essence, or what it is that makes Him what He is. But His attributes are the ways in which God manifests His essence to His creation and makes Himself knowable by us.

The Attributes of God

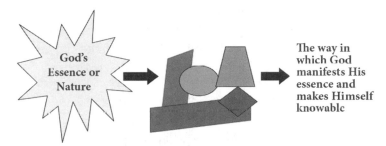

Difficulty in Classifying the Attributes of God

Due to the awesomeness of God, who is infinite and perfect in His nature and actions, some have ranked certain of His attributes above others. Some emphasize His love; others, His holiness or differentness. But to exalt any attribute over another is unacceptable, for God's essence is not complete without all of the attributes in absolute unity and equality.

Another inaccurate view is that God can choose not to exercise a particular attribute, or to exercise it less than another. Such cannot be the case. For example, one might argue that God chooses not to exercise His omnipotence or sovereignty in order to give human beings the opportunity to exercise their power or sovereign choice. But this is saying that God can cease to be God, since without each of His attributes operating in total unity and perfection, not merely latent, He is not God. The essence of God is what makes Him God, and He cannot cease to be what He is.

Gordon Clark has expressed it well: "The divine attributes are, in the language of ordinary conversation, simply the characteristics or qualities of God. As water is wet and fire hot, so God is eternal, immutable, omnipotent, just, holy, and so on. Perhaps these divine characteristics are quite numerous; but usually it is only the more comprehensive terms that are discussed."[6]

In discussing God's attributes, we have used terms like characteristics, properties, qualities, and attributes. They all mean the same thing. The idea is to try to describe what in fact makes God to be God, not something else. We and other creatures may share aspects of the divine nature in finite proportion and imperfection, but God is all that He is infinitely, perfectly, and entirely.

Attributes Are Divided into Two Categories

Theologians classify God's attributes in different ways to help us understand how God is within Himself and how He is in reference to the world. The first way of looking at God is called *attributes ad intra* and the latter, *attributes ad extra*.

Theologians also seek to explain ways in which we are similar to God (e.g., God is just and man too can be just) and ways in which God is unique (e.g., God is infinite and we are finite).[7]

There are numerous approaches to classifying God's attributes. One involves distinguishing between God's personal attributes and His absolute attributes, or His natural and moral attributes, or His communicable and incommunicable attributes. A. H. Strong has suggested using two categories: absolute attributes and relative attributes. Within absolute attributes, Strong lists spirituality (life and personality), infinity (self-existence and immutability), and perfection (truth, love, and holiness). Within relative attributes, Strong lists time and space (eternity and immensity), creation (omnipresence, omniscience, and omnipotence), and God's relation to moral beings (veracity, faithfulness, mercy, goodness, justice, and righteousness).[8]

Another approach is to study God's attributes in reference to Himself, moral creatures, and creation. Thus, we would study God's inner attributes, such as holiness, truth, love, immensity, eternity, self-existence, personality, spirituality, infinity, and perfection—what God is in Himself. Then we would explore aspects of God's nature in relation to moral creatures, considering qualities such as justice, righteousness, veracity, faithfulness, mercy, goodness, and graciousness. Finally, we would consider God's attributes relative to creation in general—His omniscience, omnipresence, omnipotence, and immutability.

The Attributes of God with Respect to . . .

Without minimizing what has been said about the nature of God, which is reasonably inferred from the Scriptures, it is wise to heed theologian Millard J. Erickson's admonition: "The Bible does not speak of God as some sort of infinite computer. Rather, the images used are very concrete and warm. God is pictured as a father, a shepherd, a friend. . . . The best mode of investigating the attributes of God, then, is to examine the Scriptural statements carefully and make reasonable inferences from them."[9]

8. In what ways is God like us and not like us?

We have discussed this matter partially in question five on the nature of theological language and in question six on God as a personal being. God and humans are alike in many ways, but God is also very much unlike us. The properties that God and people share are called communicable attributes, whereas the attributes that are unique to God are called incommunicable attributes.

Attributes God does not share with humans are self-existence (aseity), simplicity, and infinity. Let us take a look at each one of them to understand how they are necessarily unique to God and why we cannot share them.

Self-existence

Everything created depends on something else outside of creation for its existence, but God is an uncreated being. William G. T. Shedd rightly says, "The ground of his being is in himself."[10]

All life and creation has its existence from God. Because He is the source of all things external to Himself, He is the source of each of our lives (Ps. 139:13–16), the source of love (Ps. 36:7), and the source of all our provisions (Ps. 36:8).

Simplicity

God is one simple and undivided being. Things within time and space, such as humans, are made up of parts, and it is natural that we should believe that God is also, but this is not true. He exists outside of time and space and is not influenced by matter. He is numerically and uniquely one being (Deut. 6:4; Isa. 43:10–11; 45:5, 21), but expressed eternally in three persons, Father, Son, and Holy Spirit

(John 1:1; 10:30; Acts 5:3–4). Louis Berkhof explains simplicity in this manner: "When we speak of the simplicity of God, we use the term to describe the state or quality of being simple, the condition of being free from division into parts, and therefore from compositeness."[11]

When we speak of God's unity, we express "both the oneness and the unicity of God, the fact that He is numerically one and that as such He is unique."[12] One of the major passages that support this unity is Deuteronomy 6:4, "Hear, O Israel! Yahweh is our God, Yahweh is one!"

In contrast to the multitude of deities in the world, the true God is numerically one being. But how does this square with the doctrine of the Trinity. Unity is not the same thing as unit. Theologian Henry Thiessen says, "A unit is marked by mere singleness. The unity of God allows for the existence of personal distinctions in the divine nature, while at the same time recognizing that the divine nature is numerically and eternally one. Unity does imply that the persons of the trinity are not separate subsistences within the divine essence. Many sects and cults have broken with the historical Christian faith at this point by failing to accept the doctrine of three persons but one essence."[13]

God is not, then, just one numerical being; He is also undivided in His being. In Trinitarian terms, there is one Being who is three persons, with no confusion of these persons and no division of the being. Moreover, each of the three persons, though distinct, is the same numerical Being in the totality. There is no attribute possessed by one of the persons that is not equally that of the others as well.

God's simplicity also means that God does not experience any change in mode or time. There is no passage of time with Him, no before or after. There is only the ever-present. Moreover, there is no movement from one place to another. Time and space are creational in nature, and matter decays, existing as it does in time and space; but not so the timeless and spaceless Being who created all.

Further discussion of God's simplicity may be found in question 21.

Infinity

The Creator of the universe has no limitations other than those that are inconsistent with His nature. In speaking of God's limitlessness, generally we mean that He is unlimited in regard to His creation. He is infinite respecting time and space.

But let us begin by considering His infinite perfection. God is absolutely complete in His nature. There is nothing lacking in Him. He is all that He should be. No property is missing from His nature, nor is there even a minor defect in any of His qualities. He is free from all limitations other than self-limitation.

Thus, God is infinite in regard to time. He is eternal; he transcends time. Berkhof explains the Creator's nature in respect to time as "that perfection of God whereby He is elevated above all temporal limits and all succession of moments, and possesses the whole of His existence in one indivisible present."[14]

God is also infinite in regard to space. There are two aspects of this attribute. First is His transcendence, or immensity. As Henry Thiessen explains, God is "not limited or circumscribed by space; on the contrary, all finite space is dependent upon him. He is, in fact, above space."[15] He is not part of the created order and is different from creation in His being. He does not exist within creation, though He acts within it, generally through theophanies or special manifestations such as the burning bush of Moses or the shekinah glory in the tabernacle and temple. These are not God but representations of God.

Second is God's *omnipresence* or *immanence*. This is difficult to explain since wherever there is time, space, and matter, there is God. However, He is not within this physical universe. Since God is infinite, He cannot exist within a finite world; infinity and finitude are contradictory. Also, part of God cannot be within time and space and part not, for He is not a partitive being. He is not spatial or temporal.

In conclusion, Thiessen says, "Due to the spirituality of his nature and our inability to think in spaceless terms, [God's omnipresence] is a difficult doctrine to apprehend. However, this much is clear;

God is both immanent and transcendent, and he is everywhere present in essence as well as in knowledge and power. Whenever and wherever it is present, spiritual substance, like the soul, is a complete whole at every point."[16]

Immutability

The last attribute of God for which there is no finite, human parallel is *immutability*—the unchangeableness of God. God is not subject to change. This refers to His essence, not His actions. The immutability of God concerns His knowledge, His purpose, His counsel, and His righteousness, to mention only a few attributes. Though God chooses to act differently within the created order and in history, His character never changes. He will always work out His eternal purposes in perfect consistency with His perfect knowledge and purpose. Though it may appear that God has changed His mind, His perspective, or His manner of relating to us, the change is only apparent.

© 2012 H. Wayne House.

Charles Baker explains God's immutability this way:

> In trying to solve this problem it may help to consider the question: "Which changes, the wind or the weather-vane?" or, "Which changes, the temperature or the thermometer?"

In one sense they both change, but in a truer sense the weather-vane and the thermometer do not change. The vane always points in the direction of the wind and the thermometer always registers the correct temperature. God said He was going to destroy the great city of Nineveh because of their great sin (Jonah 3:4). But the inhabitants of Ninevah believed the prophet and repented in sackcloth and ashes from the king on down, saying "Who can tell if God will turn and repent, and turn away from his fierce anger, that we perish not?" And we read that God did repent (v. 10). This is the kind of repenting which the weather-vane does. Actually God has not changed, for He has declared that this is the unchanging nature of His character: "If that nation, concerning which I have pronounced, turn from their evil, I will repent of the evil that I thought to do unto them" (Jer. 18:8).[17]

Further discussion of God's immutability may be read in question 13.

9. Has God always existed? (Eternity)

The God of the Bible transcends time. Since He is a simple being, He does not experience a progression of moments (2 Peter 3:8; Isa. 57:15).[18] Not only does He know the end from the beginning, He exists beyond the end and was before the beginning (Pss. 90:2; 102:27). Eternity exists in Him (Heb. 1:12; 1 Tim. 1:17).

Berkhof explains the eternity of God as "That perfection of God whereby He is elevated above all temporal limits and all succession of moments, and possesses the whole of His existence in one indivisible present."[19] Such an idea is outside of our experiences and beyond our comprehension, but as we explained in question eight, the God of the Bible is self-existent. Everything that is not God is His creation, a finite reality that was created out of nothing by an act of His will and is wholly dependent on Him (Rom. 11:36). He was before it and is above it (Gen. 21:33; Deut. 33:27; Pss. 90:2; 102:11–12; Rom. 1:20).

Even though God is above time, this does not mean that He does not have a logical order in his mind and decisions for everything outside of Himself. Moreover, His existence above the temporal does not mean that He is uninterested or uninvolved in what occurs within time. He is most interested, since in eternity He decided how He would involve Himself in human affairs. E. L. Mascall elucidates that a God who is timeless and whose world is eternally present is more concerned about the world than a being that exists within His world, since the latter kind of deity would be restricted to each moment while the former would be embracing every act of his creatures.[20]

One must distinguish between God's *existence* within time and His *acts* within time. God is immanent within human history and has chosen to act within the time and space universe. More than any other religion, Christianity has taught that God enters into our history. By means of temporal manifestations, He revealed Himself to Adam and Eve in the garden, to Abraham, to Moses, and to other prophets in the Old Testament. He reveals Himself most fully, however, in His incarnation. God became part of our human existence by becoming one of us in the person of the Son, experiencing our weakness, and finally dying as a man.

In the third chapter of Exodus, we observe God's theophany (that is, His physical manifestation) to Moses in a bush that burned but was not consumed. After God tells Moses of his assignment on behalf of the children of Israel, Moses replies that the Israelites will want to know God's name (His character or attributes). God responds that He is the "I AM" (*ehyeh*, a derivation of *hayah*, "to be), the Eternally Present One. Then God tells Moses to tell the people of Israel that He is to be called Yahweh, also a derivation of "to be" which probably means, "He is."

Yahweh, then, is an affirmation of who God is and what kind of God He is. Some have extended the meaning to, "He will be" faithful to His people. Certainly the latter is true and cannot be separated from God's character, though the former is most likely correct. Consider Ronald Allen's poignant words about the characterization of God in the meaning of I AM:

In the words I AM . . . God asserts in the strongest means possible in human language his absolute being. He exists dependent upon nothing or no one excepting his own will. "I AM!" No one can say those words in the sense of Exodus 3:14 excepting God himself. The creator of the universe is the only personality who does not depend upon the universe for his existence.

We must insist, however, that the words I AM refer not to static being but to *active* existence. All of the biblical descriptions of the glory of God are dynamic in nature. Never is God immobile, passive, static—rather he is charged with his own life, power, and dynamic. When God says of himself, "I AM," he speaks of his active existence, pulsing with power and throbbing with life.[21]

Yes, God is eternal, outside of time and space and history, but He is also present and has promised to be with us forever, which is the most important aspect of this matter of eternity for believers.

10. Does God know everything? (Omniscience)

The word *omniscience* comes from the Latin terms *omni* (meaning "all") and *scientia* (meaning "knowledge"). When we speak of God as having all knowledge, we mean that God knows everything past, present, and future, both actual and contingent.[22]

Furthermore, because God has no imperfection, His omniscience must be immediate rather than discursive. He knows all of eternity in one timeless moment, with no succession of thoughts. Certainly in God's mind, there are distinctions of events in time and He knows their logical relationship and progression. But since He knows the end from the beginning, He does not anticipate the reality or certitude of events, nor does He experience them in a temporal manner.

Even though God knows everything, His pre-knowledge (or prescience) is not causative; it should not be confused with the predetermining will of God. For example, if a person were to observe an accident occurring, the person would not necessarily be the cause of the accident. God is able to know with certainty how human beings will act, including their evil acts, without causing those acts. Only if God wants the acts to occur in a particular way, according to His own will, would it be necessary for Him to predetermine the acts. God can intervene in human history to guarantee that the events He determined from eternity will occur. On the other hand, He can choose not to intervene if an event performed by the free acts of His creatures or by natural laws are the results God desires without His needing to cause them. He need only refrain from acting in those instances to fulfill His predetermined will. Thus, all things occur by the eternal decision of God so that He may know for certain all things within and outside of Himself, either by directly causing events or by allowing events to occur that fulfill His plan.

Because God is inherently truthful, He knows Himself and His creation in an ultimate sense. Neither His nature nor creation can be anything other than what He knows eternally. Moreover, His knowledge assumes the laws of logic: nothing is illogical in God or in what He decides to do, and consequently in what He knows to be true.[23]

A recent heresy circulating in evangelical Christianity asserts that God does not know the future. This strikes at the very heart of the infinite nature of God. Supposedly, the biblical text has God changing His mind regarding His actions in human history. This limited knowledge, then, excuses Him from charges that He is unconcerned about human plights and that He usurps human freedom. See question 45 for further discussion of the heresy of open theism.

11. Is God all-powerful? (Omnipotence)

The word *omnipotence* comes from the Latin terms *omni* (meaning "all") and *potens* (meaning "powerful"), and means "all-powerful." God possesses the power to perform everything He decides to do without limitation. God does not acquire power, nor does He lose power when He acts. He does not replenish power. He possesses all power as a measure of His infinity. God is able to do all things that are proper objects of His power.[24]

This power is frequently mentioned in Scripture. The rhetorical question, "Is anything too hard for the Lord?" implies that the answer is no (Gen. 18:14; Jer. 32:27). In fact, Jeremiah says so to God: "Nothing is too difficult for You" (Jer. 32:17).[25]

This does not imply that God can perform the impossible or illogical or act in ways that are inconsistent with His character. God cannot create a square circle or a married bachelor or bring evil into existence. The universe reflects the magnitude of His creative power and genius, and there is nothing illogical or contradictory in the created order. God's use of His infinite power is qualified by His other attributes. Thus, God cannot lie, sin, or be tempted with evil. He cannot cease to exist or cease to be God. He can only do what is possible within the confines of His own nature, which is good, righteous, and holy. God cannot make mistakes, nor is He ever subject to reconsidering His prior decisions. All of His acts are final and reflect the perfect application of power for the occasion.

God's omnipotence is taught in Scripture in several ways. For instance, one of His names, *El Shaddai,* means "God Almighty." God identifies Himself by this name in Genesis 17:1 when He appears to Abraham to confirm His covenant with Him. We also see His omnipotence in Scripture in overcoming what appear to be insolvable problems, such as the promise to Abraham and Sarah that they would produce a son despite their advanced years (Gen. 18:10–14). In Jeremiah 32:15, the promise that fields will be bought and sold once again in the future in Judah seems impossible in view of the Jerusalem's impending destruction by the Babylonians. But Jeremiah's faith is unwavering because he understands that God's promises are faithful and true and flow out of His unlimited power: "Ah Lord God! . . . Nothing is too difficult for You" (v. 17). Speaking of how difficult it is for a rich man to enter the kingdom of God, Jesus tells His disciples, "With men this is impossible, but with God all things are possible" (Matt. 19:26 HCSB).[26]

God's omnipotence is intimately tied to His character attributes and flows from His unchanging nature, His immutability. Since God cannot change or "get better with age," His power is maximal and complete. He is "actualized," meaning that every aspect of His nature and character is maximal. Since God is infinite, His power is infinite and in complete accord with every other aspect of His nature. He is in complete harmony with Himself and thus can never abuse or exaggerate His power or other attributes.

God's power is freely available to those who love Him. Paul informs us that God is "able to do far more abundantly beyond all that we ask or think" (Eph. 3:20). God is the "Almighty" (2 Cor. 6:18; Rev. 1:8), a Greek term (*pantokrator*) that suggests complete power and authority. The angel Gabriel tells Mary that "nothing will be impossible with God" (Luke 1:37), and Jesus affirms that "with God all things are possible" (Matt. 19:26); thus, we have a sure basis for trusting the promises of God and a sure basis for biblical faith.[27]

But again, being all-powerful does not mean that God can do anything.[28] Although His power is infinite, His use of it is qualified by His other attributes, as are all of His actions. God's omnipotence is a good example of how misunderstanding can occur when one of God's attributes is viewed in isolation from the rest.

12. Is God everywhere? (Omnipresence)

The technical term for God being everywhere is *omnipresence*, meaning "all-present." This attribute relates God's infinitude to space. God is not subject to spatial limitations. In seeking to explain God's existence everywhere, we must understand that space is not a thing; rather, it is how we understand the relationship of material objects to each other.

God inhabits space. He is everywhere that matter is. However, He is not to be identified with or limited by matter. An unlimited God cannot be bound by the dimensions of time and space, for He is above them. Yet since God is a personal creator, He is near His creation.

When we speak of transcendence we are talking about God being separate from, and not identified with, the material universe. When speaking of God's immanence we are referring to the nearness of God to the material universe. In His transcendence of space He is not subject to any spatial limitations and in His immanence His entirety of being is at every place that matter exists.

There is simply no place that God is not in His totality. Part of God is not in one place while another part of Him is another place. All of God's being is every place, regardless of the distance between physical objects. Thiessen explains it in this manner:

> Due to the spirituality of his nature and our inability to think in spaceless terms, [God's omnipresence] is a difficult doctrine to apprehend. However, this much is clear: God is both immanent and transcendent, and he is everywhere present in essence as well as in knowledge and power. Whenever and wherever it is present, spiritual substance, like the soul, is a complete whole at every point.[29]

Christians must be careful to avoid two errors in considering the doctrine of God's immensity and immanence. The first error is pantheism, believed by many Eastern religions and New Age thought. Pantheism denies God's transcendence in that God is identified with His creation, so that God is the world and the world is God. God is viewed as the substance of all things rather than being over the universe and absolutely different from it. The second error is Deism, which denies God's immanence. God is seen as over the creation but absent from it. He is viewed as having created the universe, thus emphasizing His power, but not as dwelling within His universe.

The Bible presents God as immense in 1 Kings 8:27, where both the earth and the heavens are not able to limit Him. In fact, the heaven is His throne and the earth His footstool (Isa. 66:1). Psalm 139:7–10 speaks of an immanent God from whose Spirit the psalmist cannot flee; whether he ascends to heaven or descends to Hades,

God is there. Yahweh declares in Jeremiah 23:23–24 that He is a God who is not far off but near—indeed, He fills heaven and earth.

13. Does God ever change? (Immutability)

The unchanging quality of God's being is called *immutability*. It is one of God's incommunicable attributes—that is, only He can possess it. All creatures change; only God never changes. Referring to God's constancy or unchangeableness are other ways of describing this quality.

We can define the immutability of God this way: God is unchanging in His being, perfections, purposes, and promises; yet God acts and feel emotions, and He reacts and feels differently in response to different situations.[30]

God has existed as He is before the cosmos was created, and He will exist as He is long after it is destroyed. Although God has caused the universe to change, He Himself will never change. This has a direct bearing on His own qualities of patience, longsuffering, and mercy, even when His own people are faithless. God says, "For I, Yahweh, do not change; therefore you, O sons of Jacob, are not consumed" (Mal. 3:6).[31] Because God is unchanging, His actions toward wayward human beings are never capricious or arbitrary. His longsuffering and mercy are constant.

Psalm 102 contrasts God's eternal nature with the cosmos, emphasizing the great divide between Creator and creature. "They will perish, but You endure; . . . they will be changed. But You are the same, and Your years will not come to an end" (vv. 26–27). Psalm 33:11 stresses the eternality of God's thoughts: "The counsel of Yahweh stands forever, the plans of His heart from generation to generation."

Divine constancy has several aspects.[32] First, there is no qualitative change in God. He cannot increase or decrease, because He is already perfection. If He did change, He would not be God. This is in stark contrast to the Mormon doctrine of God, which teaches that God (Elohim) has progressed from manhood to Godhood.

Unlike the Mormon god, the biblical God undergoes no modification. Therefore, God does not change His mind, His plans, or His actions, for these rest upon His nature, which remains immutable regardless of what occurs in the universe or among humanity. God's intentions as well as His plans always remain consistent because His will does not change. What God has willed for the salvation of the elect does not alter over time because He is immutable. When Numbers 23:19 says that God is not a man, it means that His will is unalterable.

This is not to say that God does not change His present attitude or intention with respect to particular situations in human history.[33] One may recall that God was sorry He created man (Gen. 6:6) and sorry that He made Saul king over Israel (1 Sam. 15:10). If the situation changes, then of course God's attitude or expression of intention will change in concert with the situation. This is just saying that "God responds differently to different situations."[34] If sinful humanity's attitude does not change, then God will follow through with His promise of judgment; if a person repents, then God responds with mercy and forgiveness. He acts in perfect accord with His character, which flows from His immutable being.

The doctrine of God's immutability stems from the biblical view of God's stability. Some have confused this with the Greek idea of immobility and sterility.[35] God, on the contrary, is active and dynamic in a way that is consistent with His nature. His immutability emphasizes His dependability. God will be the same tomorrow as He was yesterday, and therefore His promises are reliable and trustworthy. He will fulfill them all.

There is a recent movement among certain evangelicals called "open theism." It is a reaction to a perceived synthesis of Greek philosophy and Christian theology. Open theists claim that God does not know the future because it does not yet exist; thus He is open to change with a situation as it unfolds. God is active and relational and thus open to the prayers, decisions, and actions of human beings. The problem with this interpretation of the biblical view of God is that it challenges God's ability to see the future with the same clarity that He sees the past and present. Of course God sees the future clearly. But again, His foreknowledge does not determine the free acts of free agents, it merely anticipates them.[36]

14. What does it mean that God is holy?

Some have suggested that the holiness of God is the most important attribute of His being.[37] In contrast to the incommunicable attributes of omnipotence and immutability, which are God's alone, holiness is a communicable attribute—that is, we are to reflect God's holiness. The church itself is intended by God to grow into a "holy temple in the Lord" (Eph. 2:21), and Christ continues to work in this age so that "he might sanctify her . . . that he might present the church to himself in splendor . . . that she might be holy and without blemish" (Eph. 5:26–27 ESV).[38] The church is to reflect the very holiness of God perfectly. This is difficult for us to imagine today because sin is still a reality in our lives. But we cannot ever hope to see God without being first purged of our sin nature, and that is Christ's most important work in this age.

God's own holiness is the pattern for His followers to imitate. It is a divine command: "You shall be holy, for I the Lord your God am holy" (Lev. 19:2). When God called His people out of Egypt and brought them to Himself, He said, "You shall be to Me a kingdom of priests and a holy nation" (Exod. 19:6). New Covenant followers are also to strive "for the holiness without which no one will see the Lord" (Heb. 12:14 ESV). When faced with our sinfulness, we are often tempted to despair of our own ability to reach such a goal of perfect holiness. But it is the work of Christ to bring us to this state. On our own, we can never achieve a holiness like God's. It is in this existential despair that we find the forgiveness and encouragement of God through Christ, who strengthens us and leads us into a growth of sanctification that pleases the Father.

God's holiness has two aspects.[39] The first is His utter uniqueness and separation from creation. This uniqueness is affirmed in Exodus

15:11 (esv): "Who is like you, O Lord, among the gods? Who is like you, majestic in holiness, awesome in glorious deeds, doing wonders?" We find similar expressions in 1 Samuel 2:2 and Isaiah 57:15. In Isaiah 6:1–4, we read of Isaiah's vision of the Lord sitting on His throne high and lifted up, with seraphim crying out to each other, "Holy, Holy, Holy is the Lord of hosts!" This triplet of praise is the maximum expression of utter holiness. No one can compare with God in such perfection and majesty. When confronted with God's holiness in the vision, Isaiah wailed in despair at his own sinfulness.

The second aspect of God's holiness is His absolute purity and goodness. This means that He is completely untouched or unstained by the sinfulness of the world. He does not in any way participate in the evil in the world.[40] Habakkuk 1:13 declares,"You who are of purer eyes than to see evil and cannot look at wrong" (esv).

To a very limited degree, we can appreciate this aspect of God's character. When we as followers of Christ behold any evil act, we feel revulsion or anger. Imagine how much more God reacts as a perfect and holy being. God's holiness means that He is totally separated from sin and utterly devoted to seeking His own honor, which He pursues zealously.[41] And He demands that we pursue His standard of holiness! What is impossible for any human being is possible with God.

15. What is meant by God's goodness?

The goodness of God means that everything God is and does is worthy and excellent.[42] God's goodness is the ultimate standard of what is good. It is one of His moral attributes, and it is communicable—that is, we are to reflect God's goodness in our own character.

"Good" can also be defined as "worthy of approval," which begs the question, worthy of *whose* approval? Who sets the standard? Not us. Ultimately, we are not qualified to approve what is worthy and what is not.[43] Only God himself is qualified to approve of what is good and what is not. God's being and actions are "perfectly worthy of his own approval."[44] This follows Jesus' teaching on the goodness of God when He says, "No one is good except God alone" (Luke 18:19).

What is "good," then? Good is what God approves.[45] Goodness, or benevolence, is a basic dimension of God's love.[46] Thus, God approves what is good on the basis of His fundamental character and benevolent motivation. Another way of illustrating that God is the ultimate standard of what is good and what is not good is to ask, Why is what God approves good? The answer is, Because God approves it. This means that there is no higher standard of goodness than God's own character. He approves of whatever is consistent with His own character.[47]

Jesus provides us with a dramatic illustration of the goodness of God when He compares it to that of a human father's good gifts to his children: "If you [human fathers] then, *being evil*, know how to give good gifts to your children, how much more will your Father who is in heaven give what is good to those who ask Him!" (Matt. 7:11, emphasis added). Jesus contrasts between human fathers, who are evil by nature due to sin, and God, who is ultimate goodness, to show the quality of goodness that flows from His perfect love for us. Even God's discipline is a manifestation of His love and is for our good (Heb. 12:10).[48]

Psalm 104 is an excellent example of appreciation and worship of God for His goodness in creation. Other Psalms, such as 106 and 107, provide examples of God's goodness toward His people. And Paul encourages us to discover for ourselves through practical experience how God's will for our lives is "good and acceptable and perfect" (Rom. 12:2).[49] God's goodness, then, is closely related to other aspects of His character. These are love, mercy, patience, and grace. However, it is not proper to think of them as compartmentalized within the being of God, for they all, like His goodness, are active and dynamically related to every other aspect of His nature.

God's goodness, or benevolence, is seen in the way He cares for humanity in general and even to the subhuman creation.[50] Psalm

145:16 states, "You open Your hand and satisfy the desire of every living thing." Jesus taught that the Father feeds the birds of the air and clothes the lilies of the field (Matt. 6:26, 28–29), and that not even a sparrow will fall to the ground without the Father noticing it (Matt. 10:29). Moreover, God isn't just good to believers. Extending His benevolence to all of humanity, He "causes His sun to rise on the evil and on the good, and sends rain on the righteous and the unrighteous" (Matt. 5:45).[51] John 3:16 is the great, classic example of God's goodness toward all humanity, demonstrating His love even for those who do not yet know him. Such love can only flow out of a being of ultimate goodness and benevolence.

16. What does it mean that God is sovereign?

Maybe you have heard it said that God is so sovereign He can limit His sovereignty or that He can share His sovereignty with humans. Such statements are absurd and not consistent with the biblical view of God. As Louis Berkhof says, "[God] rules as King in the most absolute sense of the word."[52] The amount of sovereignty that anyone has depends on the capacity that the person has to exercise it. Since God has unlimited capacity for knowledge, wisdom, power, and presence, He is infinitely sovereign.

Paul tells us in Ephesians 1:9–11 that God acts according to the counsel of His own free will, according to His own good pleasure and for His own purpose. Since He is perfection itself, every decision that He makes in eternity works out in time exactly as it should. Berkhof describes God's sovereignty as that "perfection of God whereby He, through the mere exercise of His will, can realize whatsoever is present in His will or counsel. . . . There is no absolute power in Him that is divorced from His perfection, and in virtue of which He can do all kinds of things which are inherently contradictory."[53]

Unlike a dependent creation, God is truly free. God's will is unencumbered by anything but Himself. Paul's hymn of praise to God expresses this so well:

> Oh, the depth of the riches
> both of the wisdom and the knowledge of God!
> How unsearchable His judgments
> and untraceable His ways!
> For who has known the mind of the Lord?
> Or who has been His counselor?
> Or who has ever first given to Him,
> and has to be repaid?
> For from Him and through Him
> and to Him are all things.
> To Him be the glory forever. Amen.
>
> (Rom. 11:33–36 HCSB)

The question is, how does God manifest His sovereignty? By exercising His will over His creation. Whereas every human action and exercise of human will is influenced by our birth, upbringing, life events, books we have read, teachers we have had, and so forth, God made all of his decisions in eternity, uninfluenced by anything except His own perfection. Berkhof indicates that God's freedom is a major aspect of God's will, which he describes as "that perfection of His Being whereby He, in a most simple act, goes out towards Himself as the highest good (i.e., delights in Himself as such) and towards His creatures for His own name's sake, and is thus the ground of their being and continued existence."[54]

W. Robert Cook sets forth a biblical view of God's will when he says,

> Will is that by which God puts into effect all he has designed. It is the faculty of self-determination. His will is free. It is independent of everything outside himself. That is, he is restricted in his will by his own character alone. With this will he endows man with freedom and yet controls his actions. His will is not capricious, for though his motives are hidden to men they are present in himself.[55]

God's will is expressed in two ways: His determinative will and His prescriptive will. Moses says that "the hidden things belong to the Lord our God, but the revealed things belong to us and our children forever, so that we may follow all the words of this law" (Deut. 29:29 HCSB). God's determinative will describes how He decides to work in His world, whereas His prescriptive will is what He addresses humans to do. God, as an infinite being, is able to act or not act in His world to accomplish His will. He also involves humans in accomplishing His plans, and when they would act in a way that would frustrate those plans, He intervenes (Job 5:12; Isa. 44:24–28).

God's sovereign will is expressed through history, time, and space. By His will He has caused all things—both objects and actions—that are external to Himself. This causation has four expressions. The first is *first cause*. Everything that is other than God is caused by Him, in that He has created everything. Even Satan and his subsequent sin would not exist except for God's creation, though God is not the author of sin. Even though Satan, and afterward Adam and Eve, freely chose to depart from righteousness, God did not directly cause them to do so, and He will eventually bring the universe back into perfection.

Second is *formal cause*, in which God determines the boundaries of everything. The structure of creation and even human capacity and choice are determined, and limited, by how God has chosen to make the universe. Third is *efficient cause*, in which God either acts to ensure that His determinative will is accomplished, or else refrains from acting, allowing humans to exercise their will provided it accomplishes His purposes. Last is *final cause*, by which God has made sure that everything works out for His good pleasure.

17. What is the veracity of God?

The *veracity* of God means His truthfulness. It is closely linked to God's faithfulness. God's veracity means that He is the only true God, and all His knowledge and words are true and the final standard of truth.[56] The basis of God's veracity is His omniscience. Since God knows all things, conformity to God's knowledge is the standard of true knowledge.[57]

The first part of our definition states that the God revealed in Scripture is the only true or real God and all other gods are idols. In Jeremiah 10:10–11, we are told, "But the Lord is the true God; He is the living God and the everlasting King. . . . The gods that did not make the heavens and the earth will perish from the earth and from under the heavens." Moreover, Jesus says to the Father, "This is eternal life, that they may know You, the only true God, and Jesus Christ whom You have sent" (John 17:3; cf. 1 John 5:20).

God, in His personal being or character, is the only one who fully conforms to the idea of what God should be. God is a being who is infinitely perfect in power, in wisdom, in goodness, and in lordship over space and time. But just whose idea is this? Whose concept of God must God conform to?[58]

Our own fallible, finite opinions certainly cannot define what the true God is like. The kind of being God is must be revealed from outside us in divinely scripted texts and in what He Himself has implanted in our minds as His image-bearers. Paul can thus confidently declare that what can be known about the true, divine nature of the Godhead is available to all humanity (Romans 1).

Our definition in the first paragraph affirms that all of God's knowledge is perfect (Job 37:16) and the final standard of truth.[59] It also means that God is absolutely reliable and faithful in His words. He can never be mistaken in anything He knows or says about the nature of reality. God always does what He promises to do, and we can fully depend on Him to fulfill His promises. Thus, He is "a God of faithfulness" (Deut. 32:4). "God's faithfulness means that He will always do what He has said and fulfill what He has promised (Num. 23:19; cf. 2 Sam. 7:28)."[60] The very essence of true faith is taking God at His word and relying on Him to do as He promised.

God's words about Himself and creation are absolutely true and conform perfectly with reality. He always speaks the truth without subterfuge or deceit of any kind. He is the God who never lies—indeed, who cannot lie (Titus 1:2). In combination with God's omniscience, the veracity of God guarantees the truth of everything he tells us.[61]

This also means that what He tells us is understandable and credible. For example, His narrative found in Genesis 1 and 2 can be trusted absolutely, even if it is not in conformity with current popular cosmologies. This means that God always speaks to us clearly and succinctly, without resorting to myth or allegory regarding the state of reality.

18. What does it mean that God is love?

The three words "God is love" are likely the most-repeated words about the nature of God ever voiced. They have been understood and misunderstood through the centuries. In 1 John 4:8 we read, "The one who does not love does not know God, for God is love," and in v. 16 John writes, "We have come to know and have believed the love which God has for us. God is love, and the one who abides in love abides in God, and God abides in him." While God is love, He is also righteous (Deut. 32:4), good (Ps. 119:68), and holy (1 Peter 1:16).

When we think of love, we think of affection and correction, much as a parent's love reflects both deep affection for a child and a willingness to correct the child when necessary so the child gains wisdom and maturity. The parent's love is self-giving, something that seeks the child's best and highest good. Love always seeks the best for the object or individual loved. Since love is one of the attributes of God, love is, in relation to God, God seeking the highest good of humans at His own infinite cost. The love of God functions both within the Trinity and outside of it in God's love for humanity (John 3:35, 14:31, 17:24).

The fact that God is love does not mean that His love functions apart from His other attributes. It works in conjunction with them in perfect harmony. Out of His love, God seeks the best for others. He loves sinful humanity (John 3:16; Rom. 5:8; Eph. 2:4–8; 1 John 4:10).

God's love for humanity is expressed at four levels:

- *Universal love* wherein He loves all people (Deut. 10:18; 33:3; John 3:16; Rom. 5:8; Tit. 3:4)
- *National love* wherein He has a special relationship and purpose for national Israel (Deut. 4:37; 7:7–8, 13; 1 Kings 10:9; Isa. 43:3–4; Jer. 31:3; Mal. 1:2; Rom. 11:28)
- *Familial love* wherein in Christ, God loves believers who comprise His church with a love surpassing human understanding (Rom. 8:35; 2 Cor. 5:14; Eph. 3:19; 5:2; 2 Thess. 2:13; Rev. 1:5; 3:9)
- *Personal love* wherein in Christ, God loves His sons and daughters by adoption (Gal. 4:4–7; Eph. 1:5; 2:4–6)

The love of God can be experienced by any person accepting His gift of eternal life through faith in Jesus Christ (John 17:3).

19. Does God feel our pain?

One of our paramount concerns as humans is whether someone beyond us cares for us in the midst of sickness, loneliness, natural disasters, and other misfortuncs of life. Whether our pain is emotional, spiritual, or physical, we all reach out for someone besides ourselves who can sustain us in our difficulty. In theology, the matter of how God relates to our concerns in an emotional way is known as the doctrine of God's *impassibility*, an attribute of God that is an important part of the classical view of God.

Some theologians have rejected the idea that God is without "passion." This may relate, however, to the definition of the word *impassibility* and in what sense it should be understood relative to God's eternal versus temporal action. After all, the biblical text provides many instances of God's concern and love for His creatures (see Ps. 113), as well as many examples of these qualities in the Scriptures. God sent the prophet Elijah to the widow of Sidon to provide food in the midst of famine and to resuscitate the widow's son (1 Kings 17:8–24). Possibly the greatest example of His love in the Old Testament is His rescue of the Hebrews from their Egyptian bondage in Exodus 2:23–25; He responds to their groaning and agony with compassion, remembering His covenant promises to them.

In examining God's attitude toward humans in pain, we must take three things into consideration. First, God did not create pain and death; they are the result of the sin of Adam and his posterity. God sent Jesus to bring salvation to those who believe in Him, first to forgive us from the spiritual impact of sin, and second to conquer death and the grave through His resurrection from the dead, securing our future resurrection by His own.

Second, we should not seek to bring the God of the universe down to our level. We must embrace the revelation He has given of Himself and worship Him for who He is. The Scripture presents Him as one who has manifested Himself to us in the person of the Son, who suffered on our behalf; but we must not try to make God in our image because of our pain. God does not flounder around wringing His hands, trying to figure out how to respond to millions of humans who find themselves in distress. God has known each and every pain of the entire human race from all eternity and has been concerned about us eternally. He works within time and space to meet our needs according to His perfect and wise will.

Third, we need to accept that the fallen condition of humanity has repercussions for us. Eastern religions deny the existence of sin, sickness, and death, but we as Christians need to embrace the entirety of Christian theology that recognizes that God will bring a resolution of all conflicts and spiritual imperfections at the end of the ages.[62]

20. Is God all-wise?

Not only is God omniscient (all-knowing), but He is also *omnisapient*—that is, all-wise. God's wisdom is the basis of all human wisdom (cf. Proverbs). God alone is infinitely wise; only He has perfect wisdom (Rom. 16:27). He alone knows which course of action is best.

God's wisdom is the application of His knowledge to achieve His desires and His plan in ways that will glorify Him the most (Isa. 55:8–9; Rom. 11:33; Eph. 3:10). His goals are the best goals and His decisions are the best decisions, bringing the best results for His desires and plans.

From a human perspective, wisdom is the application of knowledge for skillful living. For God, however, there was never a time when His wisdom was not present. Job 12:13 states, "With Him are wisdom and might; to Him belong counsel and understanding." God's wisdom can be seen in creation and in redemption. In Psalm 104:24 we read, "O Lord, how many are Your works! In wisdom You have made them all; the earth is full of Your possessions." In Psalm 136:5, God's wisdom in creation is coupled with skill such as a craftsman displays: "To Him who made the heavens with skill, for His lovingkindness is everlasting."

Such wisdom serves as a model for us (Prov. 8:30). When in Genesis 1 we read the word "good" seven times with respect to God's creation, it is a reflection of God's wisdom. For instance, Genesis 1:31—"God saw all that He had made, and behold, it was very good"—is mirrored in Proverbs 3:19: "The Lord by wisdom founded the earth, by understanding He established the heavens."

God's wisdom is also evident in the plan of redemption. In 1 Corinthians 1:21–24 we read, "For since in the wisdom of God the world through its wisdom did not come to know God, God was well-pleased through the foolishness of the message preached to save those who believe. For indeed Jews ask for signs and Greeks search for wisdom; but we preach Christ crucified, to Jews a stumbling block and to Gentiles foolishness, but to those who are the called, both Jews and Greeks, Christ the power of God and the wisdom of God."

Among the reasons we study the attributes of God are to more fully understand Him and to worship Him. The more we meditate on God's wisdom, the more we are able to praise Him for all He has done in creation, in His plan of salvation, and in each of our lives. Thus the apostle Paul's words in Romans 11:33–36: "Oh, the depth of the riches both of the wisdom and knowledge of God! How unsearchable are His judgments and unfathomable His ways! For who has known the mind of the Lord, or who became His counselor? Or who has first given to Him that it might be paid back to him again? For from Him and through Him and to Him are all things. To Him be the glory forever. Amen."

21. What do we mean when we say that God is one? (Simple being)

When we speak of God as being one, a couple of ideas may be involved. The famous Shema (name) of Deuteronomy 6:4 may be in view: "Hear, O Israel! Yahweh is our God, Yahweh is one."

The Shema distinguishes the single number of the God of Israel from the polytheism believed by peoples throughout the ancient Near East and Mediterranean world of the time. Almost certainly, though, something more is also involved. The attribute of unity says that God is numerically one; thus the Shema excludes any other beings from possessing the attributes of true deity (cf. 1 Cor. 8:4–5) But this exclusion of multiple divine beings does not argue against the Trinity, in which three persons share in totality the divine being of God.

This leads us to another matter pertaining to God's oneness: the doctrine of simplicity. God is not only numerically one; He is also qualitatively one. There is no possibility of His being divided. Thus, when we speak of God as one, we are also referring to His simplicity. God is one being—a simple being, the opposite of complex. He is not made of parts; He is of one substance.

God is "uncompounded, incomplex, indivisible, in contrast, for example, to man."[63] Consequently, God's attributes are not things that are added to His essence; they *are* His essence. Studying those attributes does not imply that they exist or operate separately. Scripture never singles out one attribute as more important than the others. Every attribute is just as true of God as any other. To say that God is holy, for instance, neither ignores nor negates all of His other divine attributes. Again, John can say that God is light

(1 John 1:5) and then a little later say that God is love (1 John 4:8). Nothing suggests that one part of Him is light and another part love, or that He is partly light and partly love; both of these qualities are at all times true of God in His entirety.[64]

All creatures are complex beings. We are made of parts. But God is not; He is the highest order of being, or simple. Yet we find different attributes that make up His being in operation at different times.[65]

The religion of Israel was rigorously monotheistic. God's unity was revealed to Israel in many ways at various times in their history. In the Decalogue, for example, God declared that "you shall have no other gods before me" (Exod. 20:2–3). Having demonstrated His unique reality by delivering Israel from Egyptian bondage, He would not tolerate the worship of any false god but demanded Israel's exclusive devotion and worship. There were no others who had any claim to deity.[66]

God is spirit, and spirit is not complex but simplex. When Jesus spoke to the woman at the well in Samaria, He told her that God is spirit (John 4:24), "and those who worship Him must worship in spirit and truth." Jesus thus revealed to the woman that God is not limited to time and space, or to this temple or that mountain to worship, because as spirit, God is everywhere. Christ makes true worship of God a matter of the heart, not location.

When we say that God is simple and spirit, we are saying that He is incorporeal. There is no matter in His being. Matter exists only in corporeal beings like us. God's unity is another way of saying that He is one spirit and utterly simple. He does exhibit different attributes more prominently than others at various times. But when Scripture speaks of God's many different attributes, it is because we cannot comprehend the entirety of God's character all at once. We must learn of it from different perspectives over time.[67]

22. What is meant by God's spirituality?

The Lord Jesus says in John 4:24 that God is spirit, and because of this, those who worship God must worship Him in spirit. The statement is not intended to convey that God is a spirit among other spirits, but that qualitatively He is spirit in contrast to flesh. W. Robert Cook states:

> It should be noted that *pneuma* (spirit) is anarthrous, emphasizing the nature or quality of 'spirit' rather than the personal identity of 'a spirit.' This is not a statement to the effect that God is of that genre of beings known as spirits. It is not a reference, therefore, to the Holy Spirit. . . . This is an affirmation that God is transcendent, pure person (in contrast to one who is a compound of matter and spirit or that which is only matter and therefore finite). He is unlimited by space and time and must be understood in spiritual terms.[68]

Based on Messiah Jesus' statement about His Father, we should understand that our true communication with God is a spiritual act and not merely a physical one. We relate to the physical world by physical means, but even when we pray with our human vocal chords, the true worship must come from within us. Being spirit, God is other than the physical world. He is immaterial and invisible.

Years ago, a Russian cosmonaut declared that from his vantage point in space, he looked around and saw no god. His statement reveals more than ignorance of the nature of God. It accentuates how all of us act at times because God is not evident to us. Nevertheless, He is there despite our inability to perceive Him through our senses.

The subject of God's spirituality flows naturally from our discussion of His simplicity. What is God made of? Does God possess any matter in His being—perhaps a very fine spiritual substance (as Tertullian wondered)? Is God pure energy? Or pure thought? Is He the "Force"?

The Scriptures reveal that none of the above applies to God. Rather, "God is spirit" (John 4:24). This word, spirit, is not used to describe His character, or an attribute, but His very being. As pure spirit, God is incorporeal, not made up of any matter at all. He is utterly "not us"—not in any way a creature (a created being).

Because God is spirit, He is not limited to spatial location.[69] Thus, true worship depends on one's inner, spiritual condition. God does not possess size, or dimensions, or mass, or weight, even in infinite categories.[70] Nor should we think of God as infinitely large, since this would ascribe a corporeal quality to a simplex being who has no "largeness." It is not *part* of God that is everywhere, but *all* of God that is everywhere.

As a spirit, God is living, albeit without physical life. God has life in Himself (see question 8 on self-existence). He is the source for His own existence and also the source of all that is external to Him. As Paul said on the Aeropagus, "In Him we live, and move, and have our being" (Acts 17:28 KJV).

Moreover, God is a personal being. He is self-conscious and self-determining, which means He has an intellect, emotions, and a will. One may observe each of these aspects of God's personhood throughout Scripture. He produces Scripture and interacts with His creation, making plans and completing them. His attributes of all-knowledge, all-wisdom, and truthfulness establish His intellectual dimension. He reveals emotion in His moral attributes such as love, mercy, and longsuffering. His attribute of will may be seen by the exercise of His sovereignty, in which He acts according to the counsel of His own will, and the sovereign use of His power.

Numerous passages throughout the Old Testament speak of God's hands, feet, and other human features. These are merely anthropomorphisms, literary attempts to describe truths about God through human analogies.[71] Because we cannot think about God in purely spiritual terms, we require a scaffolding of thought that allows us to imagine the truths and acts of God in human terms. (This is not the same thing as idolatry.) Scripture even records occasions when God appeared on earth in physical form, particularly in the Old Testament. These are *theophanies*—temporary manifestations of God in human or other forms.

But God's *total essence* can never be seen by us. This is why our heavenly Father has allowed hundreds of analogies taken from our human lives and the created order as illustrations of His character. These serve to reveal Him to us in a limited, somewhat "visible" way.[72]

Because God is not comprised of matter, He does not possess a physical nature. Some early church fathers wondered whether God was made up of a fine spiritual substance not visible to the naked eye.[73] But this speculation was unusual, and most held to the incorporeal nature of God's being. He should not be thought of as either very large or very small, since He cannot be rightly thought of in terms of space. Rather, we are allowed to think of Him as spirit. This is approved, since we are forbidden by Him to think of His *very being* as similar to anything within the created order (Exod. 20:4–6). God as incorporeal and spiritual is thereby invisible (John 1:18; 1 Tim. 1:17; 6:15–16). He is not visible to the naked eye or to any instrument devised by man. As a spiritual being, God is indestructible, which is not true of material nature.[74] Under heaven, in all the vast array of humanly devised religious pluralism, there is no one like Him.

23. What does it mean for God to be longsuffering?

God is patient and persistent. To say that God is longsuffering means He is patient toward humanity, especially with respect to punishing sin. Longsuffering is an attribute that works in conjunction with God's mercy and grace. Thus David the psalmist says in Psalm 103:8: "The Lord is compassionate and gracious, slow to anger and abounding in lovingkindness."

The Bible frequently speaks of the patience of God with respect to the judgment of sin. In 1 Peter 3:20, Peter reminds his readers of the patience of God in the days of Noah (cf. Gen. 6). In 1 Timothy 1:16, Paul states he has been shown patience as an example to others: "Yet for this reason I found mercy, so that in me as the foremost, Jesus Christ might demonstrate His perfect patience as an example for those who would believe in Him for eternal life."

Other prominent passages that speak of God's longsuffering include these:

> Then the Lord passed by in front of him and proclaimed, "The Lord, the Lord God, compassionate and gracious, slow to anger, and abounding in lovingkindness and truth . . ." (Exod. 34:6)

> But You, O Lord, are a God merciful and gracious,
> slow to anger and abundant in lovingkindness and truth.
> (Ps. 86:15)

> Or do you think lightly of the riches of His kindness and tolerance and patience, not knowing that the kindness of God leads you to repentance? (Rom. 2:4)

> What if God, although willing to demonstrate His wrath and to make His power known, endured with much patience vessels of wrath prepared for destruction? (Rom. 9:22)

> The Lord is not slow about His promise, as some count slowness, but is patient toward you, not wishing for any to perish but for all to come to repentance. (2 Peter 3:9)

Not only is God longsuffering, but Christians are instructed to be likewise. In James 1:19, we read, "Everyone must be quick to hear, slow to speak and slow to anger." The apostle Paul tells Christians that they are to lead lives "with all humility and gentleness, with patience, showing tolerance for one another in love" (Eph. 4:2). Peter encourages those who are suffering to be patient in suffering as was Jesus Christ (1 Peter 2:20–21). Finally, James encourages readers, "You too be patient; strengthen your hearts, for the coming of the Lord is near" (James 5:8).

In a world where we often wonder what God is doing or why sin seems to go unpunished, we must pause and remember the patience of God. "The Christian knows that God is not merely 'sitting it out,' abandoning us to our own devices, condemning us to a game of cosmic chance, or leading us to an uncertain outcome."[75] God is on His timetable, not ours, and He will act decisively in human history at His appointed time.

24. What is God's mercy?

God's mercy (lovingkindness) is God's goodness exercised on behalf of the need of His creatures (Ps. 86:5; 2 Cor. 1:3). It is God showing tenderhearted compassion toward miserable, needy people whom He loves and refraining from bringing on fallen people what they deserve (Exod. 3:7; Ps. 103:13; Matt. 9:36). It is goodness directed at the miserable and helpless. It is not feelings or emotion, but, rather connotes compassion and love and is expressed by God in tangible ways such as in salvation. It is intrinsic to the nature of God. It is not based on any action or trait of the individual to whom it is shown. Mercy is a synonym of compassion related to the love of God. That God is merciful is attested in passages such as:

For the Lord your God is a compassionate God. (Deut. 4:31)

But You, O Lord, are a God merciful and gracious,
slow to anger and abundant in lovingkindness and truth.
(Ps. 86:15)

But God, being rich in mercy, because of His great love with which He loved us, even when we were dead in our transgressions, made us alive together with Christ (by grace you have been saved). (Eph. 2:4–5)

We count those blessed who endured. You have heard of the endurance of Job and have seen the outcome of the

Lord's dealings, that the Lord is full of compassion and is merciful. (James 5:11)

In 2 Corinthians 1:3, the apostle Paul writes, "Blessed be the God and Father of our Lord Jesus Christ, the Father of mercies and God of all comfort." Unlike human mercy, the mercy of God is never exhausted: "The Lord's lovingkindnesses indeed never cease, for His compassions never fail" (Lam. 3:22). God is sensitive to the afflictions of our lives and provides the measure of comfort needed in each situation.

25. What is God's grace?

The grace of God is that attribute whereby He shows humans undeserved favor stemming from His love and tempered by His justice and holiness (Rom. 5:8; Eph. 2:8). In God's attribute of grace, He supplies those He loves with undeserved favors according to their need (Exod. 34:6; Eph. 1:5–8; Titus 2:11). Grace is a gift freely given by God (Rom. 3:23–24). Because grace is part of God's being, we have and experience grace from Him (Rom. 5:15; 2 Cor. 8:9; Rom. 11:5–6; Eph. 2:8–9). God's grace is always freely given by Him; it is never bestowed out of obligation (Exod. 33:19 and quoted in Rom. 9:15).

What then is the difference between the mercy of God and the grace of God? God's mercy is directed toward those who are in distress, but His grace is His attitude toward those who are ungodly and sinful. An example of this is seen in 2 Samuel 24:14, where David, in distress, cries to God for mercy: "Then David said to Gad, "I am in great distress. Let us now fall into the hand of the Lord for His mercies are great, but do not let me fall into the hand of man." Grace is when God acts on our behalf though we do not deserve it. Mercy occurs when God does not punish us though we deserve it.

26. What about the problem of God and evil?

"Why, God?"
Where is God in a world filled with evil, trauma, and tragedy?

Illness, natural disasters, murder, genocide, rape, abuse, famines, accidents, and other horrible events and conditions that occur daily across the world make us cry out for a divine response.

For centuries, philosophers, theologians, and everyday people have struggled to resolve the paradox of God and evil. Sometimes known as *theodicy*, such attempts strive to reconcile the presence of evil in the world with the existence of an all-loving, all-powerful, and all-knowing God. The term *theodicy*, derived from combining Greek words for "god" and "justice," was coined in 1710 by German philosopher Gottfried Leibniz (1646–1716) in his work *Theodicy: Essays on the Goodness of God, the Freedom of Man, and the Origin of Evil*. The purpose of the essays in his book was to show that the presence of evil in the world does not conflict with the goodness of God.

Much has been written on God and evil from all perspectives. The pantheist, who believes God is part of everything material and immaterial, holds that God exists but evil does not exist. The atheist, who denies the existence of God, argues that evil exists but not God. And the theist (including the Christian) argues that both God and evil exist, but God is not the author of evil and will one day rectify all evil.

How do Christians answer this vexing issue? If through God's providence all that occurs in the world is caused by God, then does God cause the evil that we experience?

Part of the answer to the problem of evil lies in its very nature. Why do we recognize evil as evil? Only because there is an eternal standard for what is good—God. In his book *Mere Christianity,* first presented as a series of radio broadcasts during World War II, Christian apologist C. S. Lewis declared that when he was an atheist, "my argument against God was that the universe seemed so cruel and unjust. But how had I got this idea of *just* and *unjust*? A man does not call a line crooked unless he has some idea of a straight line."[76]

Christianity holds that God is indeed good and that evil also exists. It also contends that only an all-good and all-powerful God can and will eliminate evil. Evil is not a thing or substance in and of itself, because we know that God created all things and declared them good (Gen. 1:1, 31; 1 Tim. 4:4). Rather, evil is a privation of good. It is a lack or corruption of good, like rust to iron or moth holes to wool.

God is sovereign and in control of the world (Job 42:2; Pss. 115:3; 135:6), but that does not mean that He is the author of evil. Norman Geisler writes,

> Nevertheless, note that the word *author* is being used in two different senses. Yes, God is the author of everything, including evil, in the sense that He *permits* it, but not in the sense that He *produces* it. Evil happens in His *permissive* will, but He does not promote evil in His *perfect* will. God allows evil yet does not encourage it. Just like parents give limited freedom to their children to learn from their mistakes, even so God does with His children. But in no way does God "author" evil in the sense of producing, promoting, or performing it. Indeed, God is "of purer eyes than to see evil and cannot look at wrong" (Hab. 1:13 ESV).[77]

Evil originates in the free will (given by God to humans) and actions of individuals who choose to follow personal desires rather than God's plan for humanity. It is part of the fallen nature of creation and the sinful nature of all humans. God will one day eradicate all evil (Rom. 8:18–21; Rev. 21:1–5).

This does not mean that we always understand evil, nor does it mean that we can diminish the effects of evil in our lives and the world around us. We cannot make sense of it all, but an omniscient God can, and He has a purpose for everything—including evil. There are good purposes, some of which we know and some of which we do not know.

Some evil can be labeled as moral evil. It stems directly from the actions of an individual. There is also physical evil. This evil is the type that includes natural disasters. It might be easier to explain the former than the latter with respect to God.

What are we to say about physical evil? Even here it can be argued that physical evil is in some way related to the free will of individuals, either now or in the past such as the sin of Adam. Geisler summarizes this response with ten very helpful statements:

- Some physical evil is directly self-inflicted.
- Some physical evil is an indirect result of free choice.
- Some physical evil is the direct result of the free choices of others.
- Some physical evil is the indirect result of the free choices of others.
- Some physical evil is the byproduct of a good process.
- Some physical evil is necessary for the greater physical good.
- Some physical evil is needed for a greater moral good.
- Some physical evil may be inflicted by God's justice in punishing evil actions.
- Some physical evil is a result of Adam's free choice.
- Some physical evil is a result of evil spirit beings.[78]

What about natural disasters such as typhoons, tornadoes, and tsunamis? Geisler responds, "It is charged that much physical evil is not the result of free choices and, therefore, can be blamed on God. . . . All physical evil can be related to free choice, either directly or indirectly. According to one view, Adam's sin alone could account for all physical evils. Add to that the evils inflicted by Satan and the evil spirits and one need look no further for the possible explanation of all physical evil."[79]

No single argument or presentation is going to satisfy every skeptic (or Christian) with respect to evil and the problem of pain and suffering. The questions are real because the trauma and tragedy we experience is real. But there are reasonable answers for those who are willing to listen, read, and study.

PART 3

The Names of God

27. What is the proper name of God?

Personal names in the Bible are very important. A biblical figure's name represented all that the person was in character and being. Therefore, changes in names were significant—witness Abram to Abraham (Gen. 17:4–5), Jacob to Israel (Gen. 32:28), and Simon to Peter (Matt. 16:17–18).

Theologian Carl F. H. Henry observes:

> In the tradition of the Orient, a name is not merely a vocable having its own distinct sounds and letters, but expresses the inner nature of the intended object. The ancient biblical world recognized an inner relationship between reality and language, and particularly between name and character. The name not only serves the purpose of identification, as do personal names in the Western world, but also serves a descriptive and definitive function in the disclosure of inner nature. . . . Both divine and human names were regarded as an extension of the personality of their bearers.[1]

This is important because when God chose to reveal Himself to humanity, He was initiating a Creator-creature relationship that included disclosing Himself and His attributes. In Henry's words, "The biblical names of God carry divinely authorized information about God's nature and ways, that is, authentic knowledge of transcendent Being."[2] God's name and names identify His nature. Louis Berkhof writes, "The names of God are not of human invention, but of divine origin, though they are all borrowed from human language, and derived from human and earthly relations."[3]

God has a proper name, and when in human history, recorded in the pages of the Bible, He tells us that name, the revelation is more than a divine nametag. It is an act of cosmic significance and eternal ramifications. It is the personal identity of the God of the universe.

God's name, *Yahweh*, occurs 6,823 times in the Bible. It first appears in Genesis 2:4, where it is joined with *Elohim*. It is always used solely of the true God and never appears as a name for any of the pagan gods or for people.[4] Interestingly (but not surprisingly), *Yahweh* as the name of Israel's God has been found in archeological artifacts such as the Mesha Stele (ca. 840 B.C.), the Arad Ostraca (ca. late 500s B.C.), the letters from Lachish (ca. 597–587 B.C.), and inscriptions from an archeological tomb site known as Khirbet el-Qom (ca. 750–700 B.C.) and Kuntillet Ajrud (ca. 925–875 B.C.).[5]

Readers of most English Bibles do not see the proper name of God, only "Lord" as a substitute. This is unfortunate, because in Exodus 3:14–15, God reveals *Yahweh* as the name by which He desires to be known for all generations. In Hebrew, because there are no vowels in the alphabet, one only sees the four consonants YHWH (called the *tetragrammaton*, from Greek, meaning "four letters"). However, the name most likely was originally pronounced Yahweh.

After the fourth century A.D., Christians in the West began using Latin for their translation of the Bible (the Vulgate). The combination of the Latin letters JHVH led to the English translation "Jehovah" instead of "YHWH" or "Yahweh." The different vowels used stem from those found in another name for God, *Adonai*.

To JHVH was added the a-, o-, and e-class vowels of the Hebrew *Adonai*. A direct equivalent in English, rather than Latin, would be YeHoWaH. In reality, any variation of these vowels, such as YaHeWoH, would be as good as the next, since any such pronunciation is merely a fabricated substitution for the word *Yahweh*.

The first to use *Jehovah* in an English translation was in William Tyndale's 1530 translation of the Pentateuch. The usage continued in early English translations such as the Great Bible (1539), the Bishops' Bible (1568), and the King James Bible (1611). In more recent years, Jehovah is used in the American Standard Bible (1901) and the Living Bible (1971).

An important passage regarding the revelation of God's name is Exodus 3:13–15:

> Then Moses said to God, "Behold, I am going to the sons of Israel, and I will say to them, 'The God of your fathers has sent me to you.' Now they may say to me, 'What is His name?' What shall I say to them?"
>
> God said to Moses, "I Am Who I Am"; and He said, "Thus you shall say to the sons of Israel, 'I Am has sent me to you.'"
>
> God furthermore said to Moses, "Thus you shall say to the sons of Israel, 'The Lord, the God of your fathers, the God of Abraham, the God of Isaac, and the God of Jacob, has sent me to you.' This is My name forever, and this is My memorial-name to all generations."

The name *Yahweh* comes from the Hebrew verb "to be" (*hayah*). In verse 14 the first person singular of *hayah* is used by which Yahweh expresses His own eternal nature by saying to Moses, "I am" (*'ehyeh*) has sent him to the Hebrews. He then follows up this intensive form of I am who I am with the proper name of God which is used over 5,000 times in the Old Testament, namely, *Yahweh*, which means "He is." Only the eternal God Himself can say "I am" but we may rejoin "He is." The present tense gives the idea that God is not bound by time but is always in the present and always will be in the future. In the New Testament, Jesus uses the word in John 8:58 identifying Himself as deity: "Jesus said to them, 'Truly, truly, I say to you, before Abraham was born, I am.'"

Yahweh is often compounded with other words such as *sabaoth*, or "hosts," often referring to armies. Thus, *Yahweh Sabaoth* is interpreted as "Lord of Hosts." Other compound names include:

- *Yahweh Nissi* ("my banner")—"Moses built an altar and named it Yahweh is My Banner" (Exod. 17:15).
- *Yahweh Rapha* ("healer")—"And He said, 'If you will give earnest heed to the voice of the Lord your God, and do what is right in His sight, and give ear to His commandments, and keep all His statutes, I will put none of the diseases on you which I have put on the Egyptians; for I, Yahweh, am your healer'" (Exod. 15:26).
- *Yahweh Rohi* ("my shepherd")—"Yahweh is my shepherd, I shall not want" (Ps. 23:1).
- *Yahweh Jireh* ("to see ahead or to provide")—"Abraham called the name of that place Yahweh Will Provide, as it is said to this day, 'In the mount of Yahweh it will be provided'" (Gen. 22:14).
- *Yahweh Shalom* ("peace")—"Then Gideon built an altar there to Yahweh and named it Yahweh is Peace" (Judg. 6:24).

Each of these names is revelation about God.

Wherever the Bible stresses God's personal relationship with His people, the name *Yahweh* is used. If God the Creator is being emphasized, then *Elohim* (or *El*) is used. An example of this can be seen in Psalm 19, where David describes God's relationship to the world in verses 1–6 using *El*; then in verses 7–17, David describes the relationship of God to those who know Him using *Yahweh*.

28. What does Scripture mean by the name of God in the singular?

The name of God in the singular represents "the whole manifestation of God in His relation to His people, or simply . . . becomes synonymous with God . . . in His self-revelation"[6] In the ancient Near East, a name was not just a label that identied a person. Rather, it was an expression of the nature of the thing designated. In part, this is why there was significance to the naming of the animals by Adam in the garden of Eden (Gen. 2:20).

The name of God, or "the Name (as in Lev. 24:11)," stands for the very revelation of the character of God. It is the succinct expression of all that is known about God. "The Name is thus often used for God's entire reality: it is equivalent to the totality of his attributes."[7]

Following are some examples from Scripture of this usage of the name of God:

> You shall not take the name of Yahweh your God in vain, for Yahweh will not leave him unpunished who takes His name in vain. (Exod. 20:7)

> The son of the Israelite woman blasphemed the Name and cursed. So they brought him to Moses. (Lev. 24:11)

> O Yahweh, our Lord,
> How majestic is Your name in all the earth,
> Who have displayed Your splendor above the heavens!
> (Ps. 8:1)

> I will praise the name of God with song. (Ps. 69:30)

> As is Your name, O God,
> So is Your praise to the ends of the earth;
> Your right hand is full of righteousness. (Ps. 48:10)

The name of Yahweh is a strong tower;
The righteous runs into it and is safe. (Prov. 18:10)

Daniel said, "Let the name of God be blessed forever and ever, For wisdom and power belong to Him." (Dan. 2:20)

For "the name of God is blasphemed among the Gentiles because of you," just as it is written. (Rom. 2:24)

All who are under the yoke as slaves are to regard their own masters as worthy of all honor so that the name of God and our doctrine will not be spoken against. (1 Tim. 6:1)

Men were scorched with fierce heat; and they blasphemed the name of God who has the power over these plagues, and they did not repent so as to give Him glory. (Rev. 16:9)

29. Is the name Father ever applied to God in the Old Testament?

There are several references in the Old Testament to God as Father, but there is no indication that any Old Testament person directly addressed God as Father. Among the passages are the following:

Do you thus repay Yahweh,
O foolish and unwise people?
Is not He your Father who has bought you?
He has made you and established you. (Deut. 32:6)

He will cry to Me, "You are my Father,
My God, and the rock of my salvation." (Ps 89:26)

For You are our Father, though Abraham does not know us
And Israel does not recognize us.
You, O Yahweh, are our Father,
Our Redeemer from of old is Your name. (Isa. 63:16)

But now, O Yahweh, You are our Father,
We are the clay, and You our potter;
And all of us are the work of Your hand. (Isa. 64:8)

Have you not just now called to Me,
"My Father, You are the friend of my youth"? (Jer. 3:4)

Then I said,
"How I would set you among My sons
And give you a pleasant land,
The most beautiful inheritance of the nations!"
And I said, "You shall call Me, My Father,
And not turn away from following Me.'" (Jer. 3:19)

The idea of God's Fatherhood was certainly present, but it was not as developed as it became in the first century, when Jesus addressed God as Father (cf. Matt. 11:25; 26:39, 42; Mark 14:36; Luke 22:42; 23:34, 46; John 11:41; 12:28). There are many more references of Jesus speaking about God the Father.

The concept of God as Father was developed in the New Testament as both a relationship between God the Son and God the Father, and as a relationship between God the Father and believers. With respect to the first relationship, in Mark 14:36, Jesus uses the most intimate of terms, *Abba*, meaning, "Daddy." There, we read, "And He was saying, 'Abba! Father! All things are possible for You; remove this cup from Me; yet not what I will, but what You will.'" As for God's relationship with the Christian, Jesus said that we may address God as Father when we pray: "'Pray, then, in this way: "Our Father who is in heaven, hallowed be Your name"'" (Matt. 6:9). Additionally, Paul writes in Romans 8:15, "For you have not received a spirit of slavery leading to fear again, but you have received a spirit of adoption as sons by which we cry out, 'Abba! Father!'"

30. Is the name Son ever applied to God in the Old Testament?

The doctrine of the Trinity, as presented in the Bible and articulated through the centuries, affirms that the Son coexisted eternally with the Father. That the New Testament phrase "Son of God" is used with reference to Jesus as the heavenly and eternal Son who is equal to God the Father can be seen in verses such as Matthew 11:25–27; 17:5; 1 Corinthians 15:28, and Hebrews 1:1–3, 5, 8. Although the incarnation had not yet occurred in history, Christ the second person of the Trinity existed in the Old Testament. However, the name Son as a reference to God does not appear in the Old Testament. (In Psalm 2, verses 7 and 12 do refer to Christ, but the word *son* in the passage is not of itself a name of God.)[8]

31. Is the name Holy Spirit ever applied to God in the Old Testament?

The New Testament affirms the work of the Holy Spirit (cf. Acts 7:51; 1 Peter 1:21) in the Old Testament. There are also about a hundred references to the Holy Spirit in the Old Testament itself.[9] However, as a name of God, Holy Spirit does not occur except in an adjectival sense in two passages:

> Do not cast me away from Your presence
> And do not take Your Holy Spirit from me. (Ps. 51:11)

> But they rebelled
> And grieved His Holy Spirit;
> Therefore He turned Himself to become their enemy,
> He fought against them.
> Then His people remembered the days of old, of Moses.
> Where is He who brought them up out of the sea
> with the shepherds of His flock?
> Where is He who put His Holy Spirit in the midst of them?
> (Isa. 63:10–11)

There is no question of the deity of the Holy Spirit or His activity in the Old Testament. But when the Israelites thought of God, they did not call Him the Holy Spirit as a name. Following are some of the ways that the Old Testament refers to the Holy Spirit.

Spirit of God

The earth was formless and void, and darkness was over the surface of the deep, and the Spirit of God was moving over the surface of the waters. (Gen. 1:2)

I have filled him with the Spirit of God in wisdom, in understanding, in knowledge, and in all kinds of craftsmanship. (Exod. 31:3)

And Balaam lifted up his eyes and saw Israel camping tribe by tribe; and the Spirit of God came upon him. (Num. 24:2)

Now the Spirit of God came on Azariah the son of Oded. (2 Chron. 15:1)

The Spirit of God has made me,
And the breath of the Almighty gives me life. (Job 33:4)

Spirit of the Lord

The Spirit of the Lord will rest on Him,
The spirit of wisdom and understanding,
The spirit of counsel and strength,
The spirit of knowledge and the fear of the Lord. (Isa. 11:2)

The Spirit of the Lord God is upon me,
Because the Lord has anointed me
To bring good news to the afflicted;
He has sent me to bind up the brokenhearted,

To proclaim liberty to captives
And freedom to prisoners. (Isa. 61:1)

My Spirit

Then the Lord said, "My Spirit shall not strive with man
forever, because he also is flesh; nevertheless his days shall
be one hundred and twenty years." (Gen. 6:3)

Behold, My Servant, whom I uphold;
My chosen one in whom My soul delights.
I have put My Spirit upon Him;
He will bring forth justice to the nations. (Isa. 42:1)

For I will pour out water on the thirsty land
And streams on the dry ground;
I will pour out My Spirit on your offspring
And My blessing on your descendants. (Isa. 44:3)

I will put My Spirit within you and cause you to walk in My
statutes, and you will be careful to observe My ordinances.
(Ezek. 36:27)

It will come about after this
That I will pour out My Spirit on all mankind;
And your sons and daughters will prophesy,
Your old men will dream dreams,
Your young men will see visions.
Even on the male and female servants
I will pour out My Spirit in those days. (Joel 2:28–29)

32. What is the meaning of the name *Elohim*?

Elohim is the most common name of God found in the Bible. It
appears more than 2,500 times in the Old Testament and is the first
name of God we encounter in Genesis 1:1. But the word is not used

exclusively of God; sometimes it is used of other gods (Gen. 31:30) and even humans (Exod. 4:16; 7:1; Ps. 82:1, 6). In Psalm 8:5, the word is used in reference to angelic beings and in Job 1:6 it is found in the phrase "sons of God."[10] The word also occurs in reference to deities in other languages such as Assyrian and Ugaritic.

The etymology of *elohim* is uncertain, but most scholars agree that the word is based on a root that means "might" or "power." Therefore, as a name of God, the word means "the Mighty One." Good examples of its usage as such are found in Judges 5:3 and Isaiah 17:6. Although in Hebrew the word is in a plural form, it is understood to be singular when it refers to the true God. The most common explanation for the plural form is that it is plural of majesty, meaning that all the majesty of deity is encompassed by God, and not as a true plural noun. This explanation is further supported in that the noun is consistently used with singular verb forms as well as with singular adjectives and pronouns. The biblical doctrine of the Trinity is not based on this plural form of God's name.

The usage of *Elohim* in the Old Testament, especially in the Pentateuch, seems to be a designation of God in His transcendence and as the Creator of the universe. It does not convey the idea of the personal name of God, *Yahweh*, which entails the true God's unique and personal relationship with His people.[11] However, the word *Elohim* is often accompanied by the term *Yahweh* (e.g., Gen. 2:4–5; Exod. 34:23; Ps. 68:18). It is also used in conjunction with other descriptive phrases that give insights into the character and work of God. Among these verses are ones showing God's . . .

Sovereignty

> God of all the earth (Isa. 54:5).
> God of all flesh (Jer. 32:27).
> God of gods and the Lord of lords, the great, the mighty, and
>   the awesome God (Deut. 10:17).
> God Most High (Ps. 57:2).

Salvation

God of my salvation (Ps. 18:46).

Intimate, personal nature

God who is near (Jer. 23:23).
God of my strength (Ps. 43:2).

The name *Elohim* is often used to express God's relationship with those He has chosen. More than one hundred times we find it used with names of those with whom God is in a covenantal relationship (e.g., Exodus 3:6, "the God of Abraham, the God of Isaac, and the God of Jacob").

This usage reflects a powerful God who is ready to use His power on behalf of those who are in a relationship with Him. The name conveys that the sovereign God of the universe is also the personal God of individuals.[12]

33. What is the meaning of the names *El* and *Eloah*?

God's name *El* occurs more than two hundred times in the Old Testament and is translated simply as "God." In literature of the ancient Near East, it is commonly used as a generic term for "god," or in the case of the Bible, "the God." Its basic meaning is, "God is the all-powerful One," connoting supreme excellence, power, and greatness. Thus in Jeremiah 32:18 we see the word used to describe the "great and mighty God."

The term was used by the Canaanites of the supreme god in their pantheon to ascribe him strength and power, and the Bible uses it in the same way to speak of the true God. Daniel speaks of the "El of els," or "God of gods." The word is usually compounded in the Bible with other words that characterize God, such as "God of glory" (Ps. 29:3) or "God of knowledge" (1 Sam. 2:3). This compounding also serves as a polemic in the Bible, distinguishing the true God from the false gods of other cultures and religions. Thus, in Psalm 31:5, we read of God as "God of truth." The God of the Bible is the true God. "The false religions only stammer God's true name."[13]

In Joshua 3:10, the word is used to describe God as "the living God" (see also 1 Sam. 17:26, 36; 2 Kings 19:4, 16; Pss. 42:2; 84:2). Similarly, probably to prevent an attitude of overfamiliarity with God because of the frequent usage of the word in the Semitic world, we read in Isaiah 45:15 "Truly, You are a God who hides Himself," implying that God is known only by self-revelation. Yet God Himself sees and knows all, as affirmed by the use of *El* in Genesis 16:13: "Then [Hagar] called the name of Yahweh who spoke to her, 'You are a God who sees.'"

In Exodus 34:6, we find the word used of God and then coupled with some of the attributes by which God is to be known: "The Lord, the Lord God, compassionate and gracious, slow to anger, and abounding in lovingkindness and truth."

Often, *El* is used to describe the personal relationship between God and the one who follows Him. Thus we find such expressions as:

> I am the God of Bethel (Gen. 31:13).
> God of my life (Ps. 42:8).
> God my rock (Ps. 42:9).
> God is my salvation (Isa. 12:2).

Each of these, like a single facet of a multifaceted diamond, shows one of the many attributes and actions of God coupled with the single word *El*.

Closely related to *El* is the name *Eloah*, which occurs primarily in the poetical writings of the Old Testament and is used to express the incomparable character of God. Thus, Isaiah 44:8 records God's words, "Is there any God besides Me?" and in 2 Samuel 22:32, David asks, rhetorically, "For who is God, besides Yahweh?"

34. What is the meaning of *El Shaddai*?

El Shaddai is the name of God that means "God Almighty." It occurs seven times in the longer form (Gen. 17:1; 28:3; 35:11; 43:14; 48:3; Exod. 6:3; Ezek. 10:5 and more often in the shorter form *Shaddai*. The latter appears thirty-one times in Job alone and also in Ruth 1:21; Psalms 91:1 and 68:14; Isaiah 13:6; Ezekiel 1:24; and Joel 1:15. The collective strength of these passages presents a name in which God is all-powerful, all-sufficient, sovereign, and transcendent.

35. What is the meaning of *Adonai*?

Adonai and *Adon* appear more than 350 times in the Old Testament. The Semitic origin of the word is uncertain, but in Hebrew its basic meaning is "lord," "master," or "sir." As such, sometimes in the Bible it is applied to human overseers (e.g., Exod. 21:5; 1 Sam. 26:19), but usually it refers to God. "*Adonai*, coming from human lips, expressed honor for God and humble submission on the part of the believing person. *Adonai*, thus, is the name that expresses faith, assurance, security, and thanksgiving."[14]

Adonai occurs frequently with the personal name of God, *Yahweh*, and is usually translated "the Lord God." Isaiah 61:1 furnishes an example: "The Spirit of the Lord God is upon me." In later Jewish thought of the second and third centuries B.C., reverence for the divine name YHWH (or *Yahweh*) became so great that to avoid risking defamation of God's name, *Adonai* was substituted for the proper name YHWH (based on Exod. 20:7 and Lev. 24:11, 16). When the scribes saw the divine name, they pronounced its alternative, *Adonai*.

36. In what sense is God known as *Baal*?

Ba'al or *Baal* is a Northwest Semitic title meaning "master," "lord," "husband," or "owner." While there is no inherent religious connotation to the word, it came to be used of pagan deities in the ancient Near East. Notably, it became the name for the most prominent Canaanite deity, a fertility god, and after the Israelites entered Canaan, the worship of Baal and other idols became a cultural and religious challenge for Israel throughout much of their history. It was against the prophets of Baal that the prophet Elijah had his confrontation on Mount Carmel (1 Kings 18:19–40). In addition to the general prohibition on idolatry (Exod. 20:3), worship of Baal specifically was strongly condemned (cf. Judges 2:12–14; 3:7–8; Jeremiah 19).

In Hosea 2:16 there is a reference to God as *Ba'ali*, using the original sense of the word "master." The NASB translates the passage thus: "'It will come about in that day,' declares Yahweh, 'that you will call Me Ishi and will no longer call Me Baali [my Master].'"

There is a play on words between *Ishi*, which means "my Husband," and *Ba'ali*, which means "my Master." *Ishi* is a term of affection (Gen. 2:23; 3:6, 16) and is the counterpart to the term *Ish*, meaning "woman, wife." The term *Ba'ali* emphasizes the legal aspect of a husband's position (Exod. 21:3; Deut. 22:22; 24:4). God through Hosea is saying that His relationship with His people will no longer be conditioned on an outward legal commitment such as a marriage contract, but on a relationship that is based on mutual affection and love: what was a legal relationship will become a loving relationship. The New English Translation conveys the idea well in its translation of the Hosea passage: "'At that time,' declares Yahweh, 'you will call, "My husband"; you will never again call me, "My master."'"

37. Are Father, Son, and Holy Spirit names of God in the New Testament?

In Matthew 28:19–20, the disciples of Jesus were instructed by Jesus, "Go therefore and make disciples of all the nations, baptizing them in the name of the Father and the Son and the Holy Spirit, teaching them to observe all that I commanded you; and lo, I am with you always, even to the end of the age." Theologian John Frame writes of this passage, "Here is one name, threefold. *Son* and *Spirit* are on the same level as *Father*. Baptism is initiation to discipleship, and it places upon us the name that brings together Father, Son, and Spirit."[15] Similarly, Frame writes, "One name is here applied to three divine beings, coordinate with each other."[16]

The word *name* is sometimes used as a substitute for *Yahweh* in the Old Testament and *Jesus* in the New Testament (e.g., Pss. 8:1; 116:17; Joel 2:32; Acts 4:12; 5:41; Rom. 10:13; James 5:14). Note that in Joel 2:32 the reference is to Yahweh and in Paul's quotation of the passage in Romans 10:13, the reference is to Jesus.

Although the terms Father, Son, and Holy Spirit are used hundreds of times in the New Testament in reference to the individual persons of the Trinity, they are not proper names of God. They are designations of the three persons of the Trinity that reflect association and identification. They tell us something about each of the persons of the Trinity. Often the Bible compares God to things in the created order, such as a physician (Exod. 15:26), a rock (Deut. 32:4), a bridegroom (Isa. 61:10), a husband (Isa. 54:5), a light (Ps. 27:1), a torch (Rev. 21:23), and many more.[17] In each of these words, there is something to be learned about God, but none of them are actual names of God.

PART FOUR

The Trinity and Intrapersonal Relationship of God

38. In what sense is God both one and three?

The doctrine of the tri-unity of God balances two tensions, namely, that God is one in essence and yet three in person. This is not an antinomy, in which two opposites are in contradiction; it is merely a paradox (an apparent contradiction) because the seeming opposites are not understood or words are difficult to explain.

Due to error on either side regarding God's essence and personhood, several heresies developed in the early centuries of the church and are still believed today, particularly by those in unorthodox Christian groups. *Arianism* maintains that the Son is a created being and does not share the same essence with the Father. *Modalism* believes that the persons of the Trinity are merely manifestations of one person playing different roles within history. And *tritheism* says that the Father, Son, and Holy Spirit are different beings, though all divine.

Initially, as Christian theology developed in the second century of the church, the word *triad* began to be used to explain that God was three. This was a clear departure from earlier thinking of the

Deity as just one personal being, a concept that caused considerable difficulty for Christians who accepted the Father as God, but also Jesus and the Holy Spirit.

When theologians spoke of the triad God, they were acknowledging that God was three. But this posed problems for the unity of God. The Latin father, Tertullian, created the word *trinitas*, "three in one," to express the nature of God as one yet three. This position is not self-contradictory. Orthodox theologians are not saying that there are three gods who are one God or that there are three persons who are one person. They are saying that there are three persons who are one undivided God.

John Dick explains it well when he sets forth the meaning of the Christian creeds: "While there is only one Divine nature, there are three subsistences or persons, called the Father, the Son, and the Holy Ghost, who possess not a similar, but the same numerical essence; and that the distinction between them is not merely nominal but real."[1]

The Trinity, then, may be explained in this manner: Within the Divine Being there is but one indivisible essence but three distinct subsistences or persons—Father, Son, and Holy Spirit—with the total undivided essence belonging to each of the three persons. Each of the persons shares the entirety of deity, with no inequality of the essence; however, the three persons have different eternal roles in respect to each other and different functions in respect to creation. This being so, in agreement with the Bible and the universal testimony of the church, the Son is begotten from the Father from all eternity and the Spirit proceeds from the Father through the Son.[2] These distinctions between Father, Son, and Holy Spirit distinguish their persons, while the commonality of their undivided essence establishes their nature as one. Robert Cook properly says, "While the attributes of deity are held in common by each member of the Godhead, there are properties of each individual person, Father, Son, and Holy Spirit, which are particularly theirs and are held separately."[3]

39. How do the three persons share the same nature?

Arius was a bishop in the church at Alexandria, Egypt, who had a major influence in the fourth century church. Though he believed that Jesus, the Logos of God, was divine in some sense, he believed that the Father created the Logos in time. Arius sought to avoid the difficulty of explaining how two persons (the Holy Spirit was not part of the controversy) could both be one God. Arius famously stated that "there was a time when the Son was not." His opponents argued to the contrary that "there never was a time that the Son was not."

In many ways, Arius was influenced by the thinking of theologians who preceded him, including the brilliant Origen, and could not understand how the Son of God could share the same numerical essence with the Father who begat Him. To Arius's thinking, to be begotten implied a creative act in time. This differed from the thinking of Origen, who, though believing that the Father and Son were not generally equal in attributes, did believe that the Son was begotten in eternity and not in time. This became the consensus of the Council of Nicaea in A.D. 325 and the subsequent Council of Constantinople in A.D. 381, which clarified more fully the doctrine of the Holy Trinity.

The Arian Controversy

A.D. 325 Council of Nicaea	Resurgence of Arianism	Labor of the Three Cappodocians	A.D. 381 Council of Constantinople
	Arius vs. Athanasius	Basil of Caesarea Gregory of Nyssa Gregory of Nazianzu	

The three persons of the Trinity are the same undivided God. In discussing the nature of the Son in relation to the Father, some church fathers at the Council of Nicaea desired to use the Greek term *homoiousia* ("similar in essence"). Arius, however, believed the Son was a created being and greatly different from the Father's nature. Athanasius and his supporters disagreed, insisting that the Son was *homoousia* ("the same nature") as the Father.

To be the same as God the Father in nature was in fact to be God, whereas to be similar to the Father could have made the Son like God in some attributes but not in others. For example, humans and angels are similar to God in many ways, but they are not God. However, the Father, Son, and Holy Spirit are the same undivided God, sharing all the totality of the Divine Being with all the same attributes. They also dwell within each other (known as *perichoresis*), but they are not each other, though they are the same God. Jesus said that He and the Father were one being: "We [persons] are one [thing, Greek *hen*]" (John 10:30). He also said, "I am in the Father and the Father is in me" (14:10–11), a statement of their unity that Jesus also wanted to share with believers.

40. Is the Son in subordination to the Father?

Theologians and the creeds of the church agree that the Father, Son, and Holy Spirit share the entirety of the Divine Being and thus are equal in every respect. No member of the Trinity is in any way subordinate to any other member of the Trinity with respect to the attributes of God. In the debates of the church from the fourth century onward, the church fathers criticized any view that made the Son subordinate to the Father in reference to the essence of Deity. The term orthodox church fathers held

to be theologically correct was that the Son was *homoousia* with the Father—that is, the same essence with the Father.

In the *relationship* between the persons of the Father and the Son, however, the church fathers did speak of the Son being subordinate to the Father. The reason for this is that the sharing of the Divine Being is different from the relationship that they experience as distinct persons. They are equal and identical as to nature but distinct with different roles as to person. The Father, Son, and Holy Spirit have an uncreated order of relationship. Consequently, the Son was God of true God, begotten but not created. This order indicates an authority structure within the divine Trinity that does not take away from its members' shared essence as God.[4]

The Fathers did not create this relational subordination out of mere convenience or subscription to Greek philosophical ideas. Athanasius and the Cappadocian fathers, among others, based the relational subordinationism of the Son to the Father on Scripture. Though the Son could be considered subordinate to the Father through His humanity, the Gospels also reveal Him as subordinate from all eternity as well. One passage that upholds this doctrine is John 14:28, in which Jesus speaks of the Father as greater than Him. Note that Jesus did not say the Father was better than Him, which involves quality of being (and which was in fact true of Jesus in His fleshly, finite body), but rather that the Father was the greater of the two in terms of authority and the order in which the Son related to the Father.[5] Athanasius, the major advocate of the orthodox position at Nicaea, explains the passage with these words:

> Therefore the Son is also of another kind [ἑτερογενὴς] and another essence [ἑτερούσιός] from those things created, and very much is in possession of the essence [οὐσίας] and same nature [ὁμοφυὴς] of the Father. Because of this He Himself has not said, "My Father is better [κρείττων] than I," so that anyone should understand Him to be foreign to that nature, but He said "greater [μείζων]," not

indeed in greatness [μεγέθει], nor in time, but because of His generation [τὴν . . . γέννησιν] from the Father Himself, except that also when He says "He is greater," He manifests again He is proper to His essence [τὴν τῆς οὐσίας ἰδιότητα].[6]

This doctrine recognizes the equality of the Father and the Son regarding their shared essence in which neither is above the other, but it also recognizes the distinction between the persons. Mark Bird recognizes the importance of this teaching:

> How is the Father greater than the Son? Not in essence, for the Son is both God and man. The Father is greater in the sense that He has authority over the Son. This does not make the Son inferior to the Father, any more than my administrative assistant is inferior to me simply because she is under my authority.
>
> Some will apply the statement "My Father is greater than I" to the incarnation itself. With this interpretation, one is saying that because Jesus is human and humanity is less than deity, then in that sense the Father is greater than Jesus. I think this is a dangerous interpretation, because accordingly, you must look at Jesus as a lesser being than the Father—as a personal pronoun, "I" refers to Jesus the person, not simply to his humanity.[7]

41. What is the difference between the ontological Trinity and the economic Trinity?

The members of the Godhead relate to each other within the divine Trinity in an eternal fashion, known as the ontological Trinity but also the persons relate to the created order, which is known as the economic Trinity. When they relate to each other in eternity, this is known as *opera ad intra* ("works within"), whereas when they relate to the creation, it is called *opera ad extra* ("works outside"). The attributes of God that are works within God describe how each person of the Trinity works in bringing into existence the universe, as well as how they work within the creation.

Within the Godhead are certain properties by which each person is distinguished. The Father begets the Son, and the Holy Spirit proceeds from the Father through the Son. The Father is not begotten and does not proceed. The Son is begotten and is the one through whom the Spirit proceeds, but He Himself neither begets nor proceeds. The Holy Spirit proceeds from the Father and through the Son, but He does not beget, nor do either the Father or the Son proceed from Him. One might wonder what begetting and proceeding mean. When using these terms the fathers of the church were attempting to explain that the Father *eternally* is responsible for the being of the Son and that of the Holy Spirit. The Son and Holy Spirit were not created and there never was a time when they were not existent, but the Father, Son, and Holy Spirit always related to each other in these specific ways.

The biblical text reveals that the subsistence and work of the three persons of the Godhead has a certain order. In the KJV, the general formula is *of the Father* (1 Cor. 8:6), *through the Son* (John 3:17), *by the Holy Spirit* (Eph. 3:5), and *unto the Father* (Eph. 2:18). The New Testament presents the Father as electing (1 Peter 1:2), loving (John 3:16), and giving (James 1:17). The Son is seen as suffering (Mark 8:31), redeeming (Mark 10:45), and upholding (Heb. 1:3). The Holy Spirit is presented as regenerating (Titus 3:5), sealing (Eph. 1:12–14), and sanctifying (Gal. 5:22–23).

In reference to salvation, the Father sent the Son into the world as a sacrifice for the sins of humanity. The Son died for humanity in obedience to the Father, and the Holy Spirit regenerates the elect of God and prepares them for Christ.

PART 5

Early Heresies Relating to God and How the Church Responded to Them

42. What is the heresy of modalism and what was the church's response? (Modalistic monarchianism)

Since the beginning of Christianity, there have been people who have misunderstood, misinterpreted, and promoted theological ideas that were contrary to the teachings of the Bible and the apostles. When dealing with any doctrinal viewed deemed heretical by orthodox Christianity, it is important to remember that the intention, sincerity, or well-meaning attitude of the proponent is not the standard by which a view is judged orthodox or heretical.

Many of the early heresies pertained to the nature of God as well as the person and work of Jesus Christ.[1] Heresies about God arose through the denial of any one of three central ideas regarding God:

1. Denial that God is three persons
2. Denial that each of the three persons of the Trinity is fully God
3. Denial that there is only one God[2]

The first of these heresies is known as *modalism* or *modalistic monarchianism*. It is called modalism because it teaches that there is one God (correct), who is only one person (incorrect), but who appears in three different forms or modes (incorrect). In this view, there is really only a single person who is God, and that person at various times appears as either God the Father, God the Son, or God the Holy Spirit. The term *monarchian* was used by groups to affirm the biblical concept of God as the sole monarch or supreme ruler of the universe. However, in the context of the doctrine of the person of God, the term was used two ways, both of which were deemed heretical: modalistic monarchianism and dynamic monarchianism. The monarchians were trying to protect the monarchy of the one God against the teachings of the Gnostics and people such as the early Christian bishop Marcion (ca. 85–160), who taught the duality or plurality of God.

Early modalists of the second century such as Epigonus, Noetus, and Praxeas identified the Son *as* the Father. This then led to the heresy of *patripassonism,* which became another name for modalism and is the teaching that the Father suffered *as* the Son on the cross—the suffering of the Son on the cross is to be understood as the suffering of the Father on the cross. In other words, it was simply God in another mode or operation who died.[3] The view is especially associated with a third century Roman priest and theologian named Sabellius (ca. 215) and thus is also termed *Sabellianism.*

The attractiveness of modalism was its emphasis that there is only one God (using passages such as John 10:30 and 14:9). But its shortcoming was that it did so by denying the individual, distinct, and separate persons of the Son and the Holy Spirit. It argues that in the Old Testament, God was manifested as the Father; in the Gospels, God was manifested as the Son; and since the day of Pentecost (Acts 2), God has been manifested as the Holy Spirit. Modalism denies the personal relationships within the Trinity.

(A contemporary version of modalism is adhered to in the United Pentecostal Church, known for "Oneness" Pentecostalism.)

The response to modalism was swift and addressed by early theologians such as Tertullian, Hippolytus, Clement of Alexandria, and Origen of Alexandria. For example, Tertullian, from whom we have the definition of the Godhead as being "one substance in three persons," wrote a work titled *Against Praxeas,* arguing that he drove out the Holy Spirit from the Trinity and crucified the Father.

The Council of Nicaea and the creed that arose from it had, as one purpose, to combat Sabellianism. The council therefore declared, through the use of the Greek word *homoousios* ("of the same substance"), that the Son and the Father shared the same being and therefore are equally divine.

43. What is the heresy of Arianism and what was the church's response?

Arianism is a heresy that denies the full deity of the Son and the Holy Spirit.[4] It was taught by Arius (ca. 250–336) who was probably originally from Libya and became a church leader among Christians in Alexandria. Because his views were deemed heretical and were strongly condemned, they did not survive, and we know of them largely through citations from his opponents. Athanasius (ca. 296–373), his major opponent, summarized the views of Arius in his work *Against the Arians:*

> Arius maintains that God became a Father, and the Son was not always; the Son out of nothing; once He was not; He was not before his generation; He was created; named Wisdom and Word after God's attributes; made that He might make us; one out of many powers of God; alterable; exalted on God's foreknowledge of what He was to be; not very God; but called so as others by participation; foreign in essence from the Father; does not know or see the Father; does not know Himself.[5]

The decisive statement and core of the teaching is, "Once He was not." Arius taught that there was a time when the Son did not exist, nor did the Holy Spirit. Only the Father existed, and He subsequently created the Son and Holy Spirit. Unlike adoptionism, which held that the Son was a man who became divine, Arianism upheld the divinity of the Son but not the eternality of the Son, and also understood the Son to be less in His attributes than the Father. For Arius, the Son existed before all creation and is greater than creation, but is not equal to the Father.

Theologian Alister McGrath summarizes the position of Arius stating:

1. The Son is a creature, who, like all other creatures, derives from the will of God.
2. The term "Son" is thus a metaphor, an honorific term intended to underscore the rank of the Son among other creatures. It does not imply that the Father and Son share the same being or status.
3. The status of the Son is itself a consequence not of the *nature of the Son,* but of the *will of the Father.*[6]

The views of Arius were more than just words—they had theological ramifications, and Athanasius was quick to see them. Salvation requires divine intervention. If the Son was created, then the Son was incapable of redeeming creation. McGrath summarizes Athanasius's logic:

1. No creature can redeem another creature.
2. According to Arius, Jesus Christ is a creature.
3. Therefore, according to Arius, Jesus Christ cannot redeem humanity.[7]

Athanasius emphasized John 1:14 by arguing that the "Word became flesh" and that God entered into the human situation to change it and provide redemption.[8]

Arius and his followers, in support of their position, used verses such as John 1:14; 3:16, 18; Colossians 1:15; and 1 John 4:9. The passages written by John speak of the "only begotten" Son, and since for humans, "beget" entails a father's role in conceiving a child, Arius projected that idea into the doctrine of God. Though not always clear or certain what the term fully meant, the early church rejected any sense in which "begotten" meant "created." This rejection was explicitly declared in the Nicene Creed, wherein the Son is said to be "eternally begotten of the Father . . . begotten, not made."[9] The teachings of Colossians are best understood to mean that Christ has the rights of privilege of the "firstborn" (i.e., "firstborn over all creation," as translated in Colossians 1:15 in the New International Version).[10]

As a result of the teachings of Arius, a definitive and clear explanation of the distinction between the Son and the Father, in person but not in nature, was articulated at the Council of Nicaea in A.D. 325. Central to the teaching of the Nicene Creed and the repudiation of Arianism is the insistence in the Creed that the Son is "of the same substance" or "of one Being with the Father." When this was put into the creed, the term *homousios,* a philosophical term meaning "of the same nature," was used rather than the term *homoiusios,* meaning "of a similar nature." The alphabetical difference is very small, that of a dipthong—*ou* rather than *oi*—but the theological difference is enormous. John Anthony McGuckin notes,

> This affirmation of the Son's birth from the very being (*ousia*) of God was a highly abstract and shorthand way of summing up the generic biblical doctrine of the Son's birth from the Father. The use of the philosophical concept of "birth from out of the divine essence" was meant to emphasize and underscore the potency of other biblical metaphors about divine sonship, rather than replace or supersede them. But in a real sense history had been made, for the affirmation that the Son was "consubstantial

(*homoousion*) with the Father" marks the very first time that a major doctrinal statement had been creedally expressed in anything other than purely biblical phrases.[11]

When the teachings of Arius were formally declared heretical, the anathema portion of the Nicene Creed declared, "But those who say: 'There was a time when he was not;' and 'He was not before he was made;' and 'He was made out of nothing,' or 'He is of another substance' or 'essence,' or 'The Son of God is created,' or 'changeable,' or 'alterable'—they are condemned by the holy catholic and apostolic Church."[12]

The pronouncements and theology of Nicaea were reaffirmed and strengthened at the Council of Constantinople in A.D. 381, with the addition of "before all ages" after the phrase "begotten of the Father" to show that the "begetting" of Christ was eternal.[13] With these declarations, the relationship between the Father and the Son was articulated in such a way that it was recognized as faithful to the teachings of the Bible and the apostles.

The technical language of the disciplines of theology and philosophy cannot be avoided in understanding some of the complexities of biblical doctrine. This doesn't mean that every Christian has to become a theologian or philosopher, but it does mean that if the intricacies of biblical doctrine are going to be understood, there will be specialized and detailed language involved. It is the same in any area of life, whether it is law, science, medicine, or computer technology.

In the words of Harold Brown, "By adopting a prejudice against the use of philosophical language and the Hellenistic influence in theology, many Christians who want to be conservative and orthodox deprive themselves of the tools that are necessary to build a stable doctrinal structure and ultimately will fall into some variety of heresy, very likely into one orthodox theology has already rejected."[14]

Words matter. Theology matters.

44. What is the heresy of unitarianism?
(Dynamic monarchianism)

Also known as *dynamic monarchianism* or *adoptionistic monarchianism*, the heresy called *unitarianism* is older than the modalistic monarchianism discussed in question 42. It teaches that Jesus is a man endowed with a special power from God in such a way as to be, in essence, adopted by God as Son (thus unitarianism is also called *adoptionism*).[15] Jesus was a man who became God through adoption. A proto-adoptionist perspective can be found in the early writing known as the Shepherd of Hermas, written about A.D. 150.

The heresy first appeared in Rome about 190, where Christians were wrestling with ideas and language to combat Gnosticism wherein Christ the Son was a purely immaterial entity. According to Epiphanius (ca. 312–403), an early church father who compiled a list of heresies up until his time, unitarianism (adoptionism) began with a man in Rome known as Theodotus the Tanner. Theodotus eventually renounced Christianity and claimed that Jesus was only a *psilos anthropos,* a "mere man," who at His baptism in the Jordan River received the Spirit of God in a special way.[16] Adoptionism continued into the third and fourth centuries with some following but never huge numbers. The lack of growth, due in part to the persecution of Christians wherein one would be very reluctant to be a martyr for Jesus if He was not truly God.

Harold O. J. Brown observes, "Their rationalistic, human view of Christ, a kind of proto-Unitarianism, was not strong enough to resist the fires of persecution; Christians had to believe more if they were to face martyrdom. The Christian hoped, in eternal life, to be like Christ (1 John 3:2). Consequently the suggestion that Christ was only a Spirit-adopted man was dreadful for those facing death for his sake; theologian Adolf von Harnack calls it nihilistic."[17]

One important proponent of adoptionism was Paul of Samosata (ca. 200–275), who influenced Lucian of Antioch (ca. 240–312), the teacher of Arius (ca. 250–336). The latter was the person who ignited the heresy that came to bear his name, Arianism, a Christological heresy that was condemned at the Council of Nicaea in 325. However, its persistence meant that it had to be dealt with at councils such as those at Nicaea in 325 and Chalcedon in 451 through language that clearly upheld the eternal deity of the Son and the Holy Spirit. Adoptionism was not specifically addressed by any of the creeds or councils, and no definitive refutation of it was made. As a result, traces of it continued into the late Middle Ages

In more recent history, unitarianism or adoptionism was held by the early nineteenth-century philosopher Friedrich Schleiermacher (1768–1834) and German theologian Albrecht Ritschl (1822–1889). German liberal theologian Adolf von Harnack (1851–1930) also held to a from of it. Evangelical theologian Harold O. J. Brown observes, "Adoptionistic ideas always arise wherever Christians are reluctant to use language and tools of philosophy to grapple with the apparent conflict between the unity of God and the deity of Christ."[18] Modalism and adoptionism both share the confusing idea of monarchianism, but they are very different. In Brown's words, "For the adoptionist, Christ is not really God at all, but an adopted man. For the modalist, he is not only God, he is the Father himself. . . . What [the adoptionist and modalist] have in common is their conviction that the fundamental unity and oneness of God does not permit a second Person to share the titles of deity."[19]

One thing the heresy of adoptionism shows (along with many others) is the importance of using language appropriately and precisely. Words matter.

45. What is the heresy of open theism?

Open theism, also known as *neotheism*, the *open view of God*, and *openness theology*, argues that God's foreknowledge and sovereignty are not absolute. This is a recent view in Christian theology, emerging in the last twenty to twenty-five years. Open theists believe that because God desires to be in relationship with humans,

God risks knowing and controlling all aspects of the future. Therefore, God does not know the future exhaustively. Theologian and proponent Clark Pinnock stated, "God is not viewed as being completely in control and exercising exhaustive sovereignty. . . . God controls some things, but not everything. He conducts a 'general' rather than a 'meticulous sovereignty.'"[20]

Emphasizing human freedom, open theists argue that there are limits to what God knows. Open theist David Basinger writes, "God does not possess exhaustive knowledge of exactly how we will utilize our freedom, although he may well at times be able to predict with great accuracy the choices we will freely make."[21] God is a God of odds and not a God of certainty. Open theists make God a divine gambler with a good record.

Open theism has similarities to *process theology*, a twentieth-century liberal theological perspective that built on the philosophy of thinkers such as Alfred North Whitehead (1861–1947) and Charles Hartshorne (1897–2000). Critics Norman Geisler and Wayne House note, "Like the process view, and unlike traditional theism, neotheists affirm that God is temporal, changing, and complex (as opposed to simple in Being). He has potential to become and does not have infallible knowledge of future free choices. He does not have absolute control of the world and is capable of learning."[22]

For the open theist, God is a growing God. Open theist Gregory Boyd is succinct in his view: "In a cosmos populated by free agents, the outcome of things—even divine decisions—is often uncertain."[23]

Open theism shares some similarities with classical theism, but there are significant differences that move it outside the realm of orthodoxy. Neotheism or open theism denies some of the central attributes of God. In open theism there is a denial of God's eternality, immutability, pure actuality, and simplicity. Additionally, "it denies God's infallible foreknowledge of future free acts and, as a consequence, God's complete sovereignty over human events."[24]

The following chart compares open theism and orthodoxy:[25]

The Contrasts Between Classical Theism and Open Theism	
Classical Theism	Open Theism
Omniscience	
God is omniscient—knows all things past, present, and future	God is limited in knowledge—knows all things past and present, but learns the future.
Impassibility	
God is impassible—nothing can hurt Him or act upon Him. He acts out of His grace and mercy.	God is passible—can be hurt and acted upon. We can make God feel pain.
Eternality	
God is eternal (non-temporal)—does not dwell within time.	God is temporal—exists within time and experiences it.
Simplicity	
God is simple—not composed of parts, absolutely one and indivisible in His essence.	God is composite—made of parts.
Immutability	
God is immutable—does not change since He is perfect and any change would be for the worst.	God is mutable—change does not necessitate imperfection.
Sovereignty	
God is sovereign—reigns over all things; there is not an atom in the universe that He does not control either efficiently or permissively. He allows us to participate in His plan of salvation but He does not need us.	God is sovereign—but He needs our help or else He will be unable to carry out His plan of salvation.
Omnipotence	
God is omnipotent—can do all things that are not contradictory. He gives but does not give away power. He has power without any limits.	God is limited in power—He gives away power and, thus, is not infinite in power.
Infallibility	
God in infallible—cannot err in any respect.	God is fallible—can err, and the Scripture states that He has erred.

There are both theological and practical dangers to open theism.[26] Open theism affects the content of belief as well as the practice of belief. It affects a person's entire worldview. "If by *God* is meant a finite, limited being, the whole of traditional theology comes crashing down."[27]

Theologically, open theism erodes predictive prophecy in the Bible, ultimately denying the omniscience and omnipotence of God. It makes all prophecy conditional upon human action. The Bible is full of prophetic passages, but if all the predictive passages that involve human free choice and human interaction are conditional and ultimately uncertain, then the Bible could not have truly predicted events such as the location of the birth of Jesus (Mic. 5:2), how Jesus would die (Isa. 53), when Jesus would die (Dan. 9:25–27), or that Jesus would rise from the dead (Ps. 16:10; Acts 2:30–31). Such prophecies must either be a reflection of the infallibility of God or the result of God as a good guesser with a remarkable record. If all prophecy is conditional, then there can be no test for false prophecy. But there is a test, as recorded in Deuteronomy 18:22.[28]

Open theism erodes the infallibility of God. If God does not know with certainty which prophecies will come to pass, then He is guessing and not infallible. Similarly, the infallibility of the Bible is eroded along with the doctrine of inerrancy.[29]

Open theism erodes the doctrine of salvation. Neotheists believe that if God knows the future acts of free creatures, then He would know which humans are going to believe in Him and be saved. This, it is argued by open theists, would violate the free will of humans. Such an argument demands that mere knowledge of an act requires determining the act, something quite untrue. That I might know that an event is about to transpire does not mean that I am the cause of it. I may only be a bystander. We would contend that the Scripture teaches that God knows the future but that such knowledge does not require that God directly causes all events in the future, including the salvation of all persons of whom He has knowledge, since this would be universalism, the belief that all people will eventually receive salvation.[30]

Finally, open theism erodes the certainty of the ultimate victory of God over evil. The Bible predicts the ultimate defeat of Satan and evil. But like other prophecies, this involves free will and thus no infallibility of God; therefore, the ultimate triumph of God and good is uncertain even though prophesied (Rev. 21–22).[31]

Open theists have a commendable desire to present a view of God that "resonates deeply with traditional Christian devotional life."[32] However, their view erodes the very foundation they desire to strengthen. Just as the principles of nutrition are applied either correctly or incorrectly in the meals we eat daily, so too the principles of theology (doctrine) can be applied either correctly or incorrectly in the lives of Christians. If one acts upon the principles of open theism, we believe there is an erosion of several key ideas in Christian life. Among them are the following:

- Confidence in the character of God
- Confidence in the Word of God
- Confidence in the promises of God
- Confidence in God's ability to answer prayer
- Confidence in our ability to test for false prophecy
- Confidence in God's knowledge of the elect
- Confidence in God's ability to defeat evil[33]

One's spirituality and godliness cannot be any stronger than one's God. Consider the following passages:

> I know that You can do all things,
> And that no purpose of Yours can be thwarted. (Job 42:2)

> Remember the former things long past,
> For I am God, and there is no other;
> I am God, and there is no one like Me,
> Declaring the end from the beginning,
> And from ancient times things which have not been done,
> Saying, "My purpose will be established,
> And I will accomplish all My good pleasure." (Isa. 46:9–10)

In Him also we have obtained an inheritance, having been predestined according to His purpose who works all things after the counsel of His will. (Eph. 1:10–11)

All who dwell on the earth will worship him, everyone whose name has not been written from the foundation of the world in the book of life of the Lamb who has been slain. (Rev. 13:8)

Each of these passages and scores of others are called into question by open theism. In Psalm 11:3, the psalmist said, "If the foundations are destroyed, what can the righteous do?" Open theism destroys the foundation of the doctrine of God and every doctrine built upon it.

PART 6

What the Ancient Church Taught About God

46. What is the Apostles' Creed?

The Apostles' Creed is one of the earliest declarations of Christian doctrine found outside the pages of the Bible. However, it was not written by the apostles (although there was a legend that each of the twelve apostles gave a portion under the direction of the Holy Spirit). Rather, it is a reflection and summary of the teachings of the early church.

Throughout most of recorded history, the majority of people could not read or write. It was important, therefore, to teach in such a way that history or ideas would be remembered. History was often taught through ballads and other oral forms. Theology and the Christian faith were transmitted through creeds and catechisms. Creeds are short statements of faith that progressively and logically summarize the Christian faith and that can be easily memorized. Catechisms are structured questions and answers about Christian doctrine and faith designed to be memorized. Creeds especially are often recited as public declarations and pronouncements of faith.

The phrase "Apostles' Creed" appears in a letter of the church father Ambrose (ca. 390), but the full creed as it is known today does not appear until the early eighth century. The creed was probably based on an earlier short formula of Christian doctrine known as the Old Roman Symbol or Roman Creed.

Development of the creed occurred over several centuries, from the late second or early third centuries through the eighth century, though most of it dates from the fifth century onward.[1] Because its development began early in the history of Christianity, the creed does not address specific christological issues that are part of other creeds such as the Nicene Creed. With respect to God the Father and His relationship with God the Son, the creed states simply,

> I believe in God the Father Almighty,
> Maker of heaven and earth,
> And in Jesus Christ, His only Son, our Lord.

Because of its simplicity and lack of doctrinal specificity with respect to the Father, Son, and Holy Spirit, the Apostles' Creed was acceptable not only to orthodox Christians upholding biblical teaching, but also to those who accepted the heresy of Arianism—a broad applicability that would be eliminated by other creeds.

Yet the creed is not universally accepted by all Christians, primarily because of questions surrounding biblical and doctrinal accuracy of the phrase that Christ "descended into hell."[2] The creed's widespread usage came as a result of Charlemagne requiring recitation of a version of the Apostles' Creed in churches throughout his kingdom. It gradually replaced the Roman Creed and gained acceptance in Rome.

Still widely used and accepted, the Apostles' Creed did not possess the specificity and nuance of other creeds and did not significantly help in the articulation of the doctrine of God. It does affirm God as creator of all that is known, material and immaterial, using the phrase "heaven and earth." It also establishes Jesus Christ as the divine Son, setting Him in relationship with the Father and Holy Spirit, but it does not discuss the Trinity or the eternality of the Son.

47. What is the Nicene Creed?

The Nicene Creed is the creed that was developed during the Council of Nicaea in 325 and is more accurately known as the Creed of Nicaea. The creed that many Christians today know as the Nicene Creed is technically the Niceno-Constantinopolitan Creed which arose from the second ecumenical council, the Council of Constantinople (I) of 381.

There had been many local councils prior to Nicaea. But the council in 325 was the first geographically broad council (therefore called "ecumenical") and thus marked a turning point in Christian history and theology. This was especially true regarding the doctrines of God, Christ, and the Trinity, with God the Son declared in the creed to be co-eternal with God the Father.[3]

The main purpose of the creed was to serve as a defense against Arianism and provide a statement of consensual belief by Christians that upheld biblical teaching and apostolic doctrine. Arius taught that, though divine, God the Son was created and was not co-eternal with God the Father. This made the Son less than the Father, contradicting the doctrine of the Trinity. Arius believed there was a time when Jesus Christ "was not," and therefore "that the Son has a beginning."[4]

In dealing with this heresy, the council wrestled with the relationship of Jesus the Son to God the Father. Among the staunch opponents of Arius were his bishop, Alexander of Alexandria, and the bishop's assistant, Athanasius. The council and the creed that came from it condemned the views of Arius and his supporters.

The creed was likely built on a template of an earlier baptismal statement. Probably the most significant aspect in the creed (apart from the appended anathemas of Arianism) was the addition of the key word and phrase *homoousios* ("of the same substance"), affirming the eternal divinity and equality of God the Son and God the Father within the Godhead. The inclusion of *homoousios* marked the first use of a nonbiblical term to define the relationship of the Son to the Father, and this term was to become the distinguishing feature of the creed and Nicene theology.

The significance for the doctrine of God and the doctrine of Christ is that the creed explicitly affirms the deity of Jesus the Son and equal divinity with God the Father. Beyond the use of *homoousios,* other anti-Arian emphases included the words "true God from true God," a phrase that rebutted the Arian claim that even though the Son is God, He is God only by the grace of God the Father.

At the end of the creed was attached a series of anti-Arian anathemas. In the council proceedings and ensuing creed, the bishops declared that God the Father and God the Son are of the same substance and are co-eternal. The Creed of Nicaea mentions the Holy Spirit and accepted it as part of the Trinity but did not pursue the nature or function of the Holy Spirit within the Godhead.

Although the creed made a strong theological statement against Arianism, it did not solve the problem. Arianism continued to spread and cause ecclesiastical and theological division throughout the fourth century. Still, the council and its very important creed were an early milestone in the history of Christianity and the doctrines of God and Christ.

48. What is the Constantinopolitan Creed?

The Constantinopolitan Creed is also known as the Niceno-Constantinopolitan Creed. It is what most Christians today refer to as the Nicene Creed; however, it should not be confused with that creed, which came out of the Council of Nicaea in 325 and is known more distinctly as the Creed of Nicaea. The Nicene Creed you may recite or hear discussed in church today is in fact the Constantinopolitan Creed.

The names can be confusing, but it is important to keep them separate in the history of the church and the development of various doctrines. The Constantinopolitan Creed is "the most authoritative common confession of worldwide Christianity."[5] It was a result of the second ecumenical council, which was the first Council of Constantinople, held in A.D. 381. Its importance for the doctrine of God is that it continues the earlier condemnation of Arianism.

It once was thought that the new creed used the core creed from the Council of Nicaea and added to it, but while the theology of Nicaea is evident in the creed, this view is no longer dominant (only thirty-three of 178 words are common between the two creeds). The creed is now understood to be a completely different document, perhaps using a previously existing baptismal creed as a framework but affirming and strengthening the work of the Council of Nicaea, which had convened a little over fifty years earlier.

The creed is very important with respect to the doctrine of God the Father, the doctrine of Jesus Christ, and the doctrine of the Holy Spirit. Each of these doctrines underwent significant development. The main purpose of the creed was to reaffirm the theology of Nicaea, strengthening the anti-Arian stance and adding doctrinal clarification on the Holy Spirit.[6] Additionally, the creed rejected Apollinarianism, the heresy propounded by Apollinarius (ca. 310–390), that although Jesus Christ had two natures (human and divine), He was less than fully human, and His divine nature overshadowed His human nature.

There are ten additions to the creed beyond the words of the Creed of Nicaea, primarily in the section on Christ. Affirming monotheism with the words "I/we believe in one God, the Father, the Almighty," the creed added "maker of heaven and earth" distinguishing God from creation and denying the commonly held pagan view that matter was eternal and contrary to the spiritual world. It is important and natural that the creed begins with God the Father and God as Creator. Regarding the use of the term "Father," Dr. Allen Ross observes,

> The creed begins its description of this one God with the designation of the first person of the Godhead as the "Father." The metaphorical language of "father" is the designation God has chosen for revelation, whether we like it or not. But we must be clear about this: it is a figure of speech; it does not mean that God is a male or a man, or that men

are more important to God than women; nor does it mean that there was procreation in the Godhead that produced the Son. The term "Father" for God is a powerful description, lofty and elegant. It should not be trivialized to mean "daddy," no matter how popular that idea may be.[7]

God is Father but also Creator, a term that says much about His power and sovereignty. Ross astutely notes,

> The creed focuses on the doctrine of creation at the beginning, and rightly so. If the biblical teaching on creation is removed or watered down, the faith will not be the same. The doctrine clearly reveals that God is the sovereign over all his creation; remove the doctrine and he is not sovereign, we are not accountable to him, and in fact, there is no basis for ethics and morality. The Bible teaches that God is the primary cause of all things. Out of his will, and by his decree, he brought everything into existence. One may quibble over the means used in all the points, but the fundamental point, the non-negotiable teaching of the Bible is that he is the Maker of everything. And he did this by decree, by his powerful word (Gen. 1; Ps. 33; Isa. 44, 45; John 1; Rom. 1; Col. 1). There is no room for natural development apart from God's superintendence in the Christian view of origins.[8]

Not only did the creed affirm belief in God the Father, but Jesus Christ the Son was reaffirmed as the "the only-begotten Son of God, Begotten of the Father," with the addition of "before all ages" expressing His eternality. This language opposed Arianism, which argued that the Son had a beginning. Moreover, the doctrine of *homoousios* was upheld with the words "of one substance with the Father." Also, the phrase "begotten, not made," countered Arian teaching that the Son existed as a creature with a beginning rather than by eternal nature.

Although the Arians didn't like it, they could accept the words, "begotten of the Father, only-begotten," that are in the creed. It was the phrase "of the same substance" that dealt them the harshest blow, excluding the Arian interpretation that Jesus the Son had a beginning and was not equivalent to the Father in essence.

The Constantinopolitan Creed expanded statements about the Holy Spirit beyond the Creed of Nicaea. The latter had simply expressed belief in the Holy Spirit; the new creed strengthened the doctrine of the Holy Spirit, acknowledging that the Holy Spirit is "the Lord and the giver of Life, who proceeds from the Father, who with the Father and Son is worshipped together and glorified together, who spoke through the prophets."

However, what is known as the doctrine of the procession of the Holy Spirit was not addressed at the Council of Constantinople. Although contemporary versions of the creed in the West include the phrase "and the Son" after the words "Who proceeds from the Father," that wording was added later, first in sixth-century Spain. It does not appear in the early history of the creed. In the East, the phrase was considered to reflect modalism and was rejected.

49. What is the Council of Ephesus?
(Mother of God)

The Council of Ephesus met in 431, primarily to deal with issues regarding the doctrine of Christ. The major concern was how Nestorius, the archbishop of Constantinople, understood the two natures of Jesus Christ, human and divine. His views, known today as the heresy of Nestorianism, taught that in Jesus Christ there were two separate persons rather than two separate natures. This is an extremely important idea, but beyond the scope of this book to fully address.[9]

The main issue to arise from the council in relation to the doctrine of God was debate over the term *Theotokos*, Greek for "God-bearer" or "God-birther." It was used in reference to the Virgin Mary and often translated "mother of God." Of this phrase, Christian historian Jaroslav Pelikan writes, "The most comprehensive—and, in the opinion of some, the most problematic—of all terms invented for Mary by Eastern Christianity was certainly that title Theotokos. It did not simply mean 'Mother of God,' as it was usually rendered in Western languages, but more precisely and fully 'the one who gave birth to the one who is God.'"[10]

The phrase likely originated in Egypt as a title for the Virgin Mary and as a Christian polemic against the pagan usage of the same term in reference to Isis, who was in pagan thought the "mother of the god" Horus.[11] Over the centuries, usage of the term spread, and by the fifth century it was commonly used to refer to the Virgin Mary. The term was popular in Constantinople, and when Nestorius became the archbishop there he wanted to suppress it, arguing that the term diminished the humanity of Christ and gave the impression that Christ was not truly human.

According to Nestorius, the term did not do justice to the doctrine of Christ. He argued that Mary was more accurately the mother of Jesus or the mother of Christ, but not the mother of God. Nestorius believed more appropriate terms to use were *Christotokos* ("Christ-bearer"), *anthropotokos* ("man-bearer"), or *Theodochos* ("God-receiver"). Opponents, including the prominent theologian and archbishop Cyril of Alexandria, vehemently disagreed, perceiving that Nestorius was trying to separate the two natures of Christ (fully human and fully divine) and deny the reality of Christ's incarnation.

The council sided with the views of Cyril. His writings were used to buttress the attack against Nestorius and were given the status of conciliar orthodoxy. The title for Mary, Theotokos, was affirmed. The result of this was twofold: first it reaffirmed and strengthened doctrinal positions on the deity of Christ; and, second, it continued to solidify the growing emphasis on Mary in some parts of Christianity.[12]

50. What is the Chalcedonian Creed?

Known alternately as the Definition of Chalcedon or the Creed of Chalcedon, the Chalcedonian Creed was the detailed statement of faith that came from the fourth ecumenical council, the Council of Chalcedon (A.D. 451). It reaffirmed ideas from the previous creeds and councils of Nicaea (A.D. 325) and Constantinople (A.D. 381) and declared that their affirmations were accurate representations of biblical and apostolic teaching.

The statement declared that Jesus Christ in the Incarnation was truly God and truly human in person without confusion or mixing of natures forever. It used a series of four Greek negative words, declaring "Christ, Son, Lord, Only Begotten, to be acknowledged in two natures, without confusion, without change, without division, without separation." While the focus of the creed is on the doctrine of Christ, stressing Christ's deity and unity with God the Father, it refers to God as perfect, existing before all ages, having a nature, producing the virgin birth, and giving revelation through the prophets.[13] Like the other creeds of the early centuries of Christianity, the Chalcedonian Creed emphasizes the doctrine of Christ, and in so doing also teaches about the doctrine of God beyond the statements pertaining to God the Father.

51. What is the Athanasian Creed?

Although Athanasius did not write it, the Athanasian Creed is named after the powerful bishop of Alexandria. Athanasius (ca. 296–373) was one of the key defenders of the deity of Christ in the early church and did much to articulate the doctrine of Christ's deity. The creed was written in Latin rather than Greek. Many scholars believe it was the work of Ambrose (ca. 339–97), a bishop of Milan. However, it may be of an even later date some time in the fifth century. Known in Latin as *Quicunque vult* (from the opening words, "Whosoever wishes"), the creed provides a synopsis of Christological and Trinitarian belief and was very popular in the Western Latin church. At one point it was widely used in the Lutheran and Anglican traditions, but that use has fallen off considerably.

The creed is divided into two parts. The first half affirms the

Trinity, dealing with its three persons and the attributes of each. The second part concerns the person and work of Jesus Christ.

The Athanasian Creed affirms the unity of God, the eternality of God, the uncreated nature of God, the incomprehensibilty of God, the infinity of God, the immutability of God, and the power of God. It declares that God is perfect and affirms monotheism, stating that the Trinity is not three Gods but one. The Trinity is affirmed, "neither confounding the Persons, nor dividing the Substance [Essence]."[14]

PART 7

The True and Living God and Other Gods

52. How is the God of the Bible distinguished from other deities?

The Bible presents Yahweh as the only true God. In Exodus 15:11 we read,

> Who is like You among the gods, O Lord?
> Who is like You, majestic in holiness,
> Awesome in praises, working wonders?

All other deities are nonexistent, and to worship them is idolatry (Exod. 20:3). Other gods are referenced in the Bible (e.g., Num. 21:29; Jer. 49:1), but their existence is mocked and they are never understood to be real. Yahweh is always presented as the only true God and "God of gods" (Deut. 10:17; 1 Kings 18; Ps. 136:2; Isa. 46:9–10; Dan. 2:47; 11:36). In Isaiah 44:24–25, Isaiah prophesied that God would one day overthrow the entire divination system that permeated the life and culture of the pagan nations. Other gods may have a subjective existence in the lives and cultures of those who worship them, but at best they are manifestations of a supernatural but created deceiver who is powerful but not equal to God.

According to the Bible, only God can save. The other gods are powerless to do so (Deut. 32:36–39). Other so-called gods may be worshipped, but they are either part of the created order (objects within nature, demons, or Satan) or the creation of human hands or the human mind (cf. Exod. 20:4–6; Lev. 17:7; Deut. 32:16–21; Isa. 40:19–20; 41:7; Acts 14:8–20; 19:23–41; 1 Cor. 12:2; 2 Cor. 4:4). "*God who is* is the ultimate Who's Who, God who introduces himself. He is the standing God before whom every knee shall bow" (cf. Phil. 2:10–11).[1]

53. Do all religions lead to God?

It's commonly said that "all religions worship the same God" and that "there are many roads to the same mountaintop." Such statements refer to the world's religions as sociological systems of belief. A corollary of them is the universal salvation of all people. Universalism holds that ultimately, every person will enjoy eternity in the presence of God and no one will experience either eternal punishment or annihilation.

There are three views on the question of all religions leading to God: *religious exclusivism, religious inclusivism,* and *religious pluralism.* Religious exclusivism holds that although other religions contain elements of truth, only one religion can be and is fundamentally and comprehensively true. Therefore, only one religion leads to God and provides the way to salvation and eternal life with God. This is the view held by historic Christianity as well as by orthodox Islam. It is also the perspective of Old Testament Judaism. Each of these three religions claims to be the sole faith, the exclusive path. According to religious exclusivism, all three cannot be the answer; such a thing defies logic.

Religious inclusivism is a bit broader, arguing that more than one religion can lead to God. According to this view it is possible that God, through grace, reveals himself and his acts in various ways and in diverse places. However, the view also holds that religious claims are either objectively true or objectively false. Not all religious claims and values are valid. Among contemporary proponents of this view are Conservative Judaism, Post-Vatican II Roman Catholicism, and modern Hinduism.

The last and broadest of the perspectives is religious pluralism. This view teaches that there are many valid religions and many life-transforming religious experiences, and each of them accurately reflects the truths of God. According to this perspective, the different religions of the world each embody different responses to the same divine reality, and each response is sufficient for salvation. Most, if not all, religions can provide salvation, liberation, and self-fulfillment. Thus all religions lead to the mountaintop, but they may differ on what they say at the top once a person is there. Among those holding this view are liberal Protestants, some religious philosophers, and adherents of Vajrayana Buddhism.

In considering these three perspectives, is important to remember that what an individual thinks or feels or wants is not criterion for resolving the issue. The best source we have for answering the question is the Bible. What does it say? What has God revealed in it? Four passages stand out:

> He who believes in Him is not judged; he who does not believe has been judged already, because he has not believed in the name of the only begotten Son of God. (John 3:18)

> Jesus said to him, "I am the way, and the truth, and the life; no one comes to the Father but through Me." (John 14:6)

> There is salvation in no one else; for there is no other name under heaven that has been given among men by which we must be saved. (Acts 4:12)

> For there is one God, and one mediator also between God and men, the man Christ Jesus, who gave Himself as a ransom for all. (1 Tim. 2:5–6)

These verses argue for religious exclusivism. To hold any other view, one must ignore these texts or else reinterpret them in such a way to include other religions. Do these verses make exclusive truth claims? Yes they do. But all religions that make truth claims are being exclusive. The real issue is not the exclusivity of the truth claim but the validity of the truth claim.

There are things that most, if not all religions, share; however, such similarities are sociological, not theological. "All religions are not equally true, nor do they point to the same destination. A religion with some truth does not legitimatize the entire religion."[2] The Bible provides adequate and accurate revelation about God. It provides truth about God. Theologian John Frame correctly declares:

> God is incomprehensible, not unknowable. He has revealed truth about himself. Thus, we are not free to roam about in non-Christian religious traditions or in general cultural experience seeking to supplement this revelation. We may use extrabiblical names for God if those terms convey authentic biblical teaching, as a means of applying biblical revelation to our times. Indeed, that happens when we translate the original languages of Scripture into modern languages. We may use new terms in order to apply revelation to our experience, evaluating that experience by Scripture, but we may not use that experience to add to or subtract from what God has revealed in his Word.[3]

We need not look for information about God beyond the pages of the Bible.

Exclusivism is not a popular term or a popular concept today. But as one author has stated, "Defending the uniqueness of Christ and the necessity of the gospel proclamation and belief in Christ does not allow for much creativity."[4] He is absolutely correct. The

Bible is clear on the subject. We may not be comfortable with it, but the exclusivity of the biblical position remains steadfast even in a diverse and pluralistic world.

54. What does God say about other religions?

God is very clear concerning other gods, and therefore, the religions that adhere to them: "You shall have no other gods before Me" (Exod. 20:3 and Deut. 5:7). The worship of any god except the God of the Bible is idolatry.[5] Exodus 20:4–5 prohibits idolatry: "You shall not make for yourself an idol, or any likeness of what is in heaven above or on the earth beneath or in the water under the earth. You shall not worship them or serve them."

In the first century, when Paul encountered idolatry in Athens, he countered it with a description of the true God and called for his listeners to turn away from idols and repent:

> The God who made the world and all things in it, since He is Lord of heaven and earth, does not dwell in temples made with hands; nor is He served by human hands, as though He needed anything, since He Himself gives to all people life and breath and all things; and He made from one man every nation of mankind to live on all the face of the earth, having determined their appointed times and the boundaries of their habitation, that they would seek God, if perhaps they might grope for Him and find Him, though He is not far from each one of us; for in Him we live and move and exist, as even some of your own poets have said, "For we also are His children."
>
> Being then the children of God, we ought not to think that the Divine Nature is like gold or silver or stone, an image formed by the art and thought of humans. Therefore having overlooked the times of ignorance, God is now declaring to men and women that all people everywhere should repent. (Acts 17:24–30)

Biblical faith has always existed in the midst of other religions, and the call to worship the true God of the Bible has always elicited resentment and rejection by some. "The pagan option is always knocking at the door of the person who crowds God out of his or her life."[6] Yet, in the midst of all the clamor, confusion, and complexity of contemporary civilization, the call of God remains clear and concise: "You shall have no other gods before Me."

55. Does a person's belief about God affect how he or she lives?

A person's doctrine of God affects not only what he or she believes about God but also what is believed about almost every other doctrine in the Bible and every aspect of Christianity. Worship, theology, ethics, prayer, prophecy, and daily living are all integrally tied to one's view of God. What we believe affects how we behave. The assurance that God exists and has revealed Himself in history and given revelation about Himself and His relationship to creation is central to Christianity. As Norman Geisler puts it, "The doctrine of God is crucial to Christian faith by any standard. Who God is in His being figures into the essentials of anything related to faith and life."[7]

How big or small one's view of God is determines many actions and reactions in life. It determines our response to the problem of evil, pain, and suffering. It affects how we understand ideas such as justice, freedom, law, and the state. It determines our view of the past, the present, and the future. It affects how we understand creativity, human responsibility, and the purpose of our existence. "The concept of God is determinative for all other concepts; it is the Archimedian lever with which one can fashion an entire world view."[8] Ideas have consequences.

Conclusion

In one of the most important autobiographies ever written, Augustine, the late fourth- and early fifth-century theologian from North Africa, wrote prayerfully of God, "You have created us for Yourself; our heart knows no rest except that it finds rest in You."[1] The human quest for meaning and search for significance touches every person. The realization of that endeavor is found in God and His love for each person. God loves you, and because of that love, Jesus Christ died on the cross for your sins (John 3:16). In John 17:3, Jesus prays to the Father, "This is eternal life, that they may know You, the only true God, and Jesus Christ whom You have sent." God put His love into action for you.

Throughout the pages of the Bible and beginning on the very first page of Genesis, the doctrine of God is present. The distinction between Creator and creature is inescapable. Everything that is not God is part of creation, and everything that is not part of creation is God. The doctrine of God is central to Christianity and a Christian worldview. What you believe about God matters—in this life and the next.

Notes

Introduction

1. Carl F. H. Henry, *God, Revelation and Authority* (Waco, TX: Word, 1976), 2:8.

Part 1: Initial Questions About God

1. We want to thank Dr. Robert Stewart for providing information that was helpful in writing aspects of this section. Much of the present question is a restatement of an article found at H. Wayne House, "How Do We Know That God Exists," http://christianperspectiveinternational.com, © 2011 H. Wayne House. All rights reserved.

2. Stephen Hawking and Leonard Mlodinow, *The Grand Design* (New York: Bantam, 2010), 180.

3. Ibid.

4. "Now by the help of these Principles, all material Things seem to have been composed of the hard and solid Particles abovemention'd variously associated in the first Creation by the Counsel of an intelligent Agent. For it became him who created them to set them in order. And if he did so, it's unphilosophical to seek for any other Origin of the World, or to pretend that it might arise out of a Chaos by the mere Laws of Nature; though being once form'd, it may continue by those Laws for many Ages." Isaac Newton, *On Optics* (London: 1721), 345. Newton

said, "This most beautiful system of the sun, planets, and comets, could only proceed from the counsel and dominion of an intelligent Being." Sir Isaac Newton, *The Mathematical Principles of Natural Philosophy*, (*Principia*) trans. Andrew Motte (New York: Daniel Adee, 1846), bk. 3, 504.

5. For an examination of the arguments for intelligent design, see H. Wayne House, *Intelligent Design* (Olive Tree Bible Software, http://www.olivetree.com), and H. Wayne House, *Intelligent Design 101* (Grand Rapids: Kregel, 2011).

6. Hawking and Mlodinow, *Grand Design*, 153.

7. See Guillermo Gonzalez and Jay W. Richards, *The Privileged Planet* (Washington: Regnery, 2004), on the unlikely possibility of scientific discovery, except on Earth, due to the exact factors present in our galaxy; Peter D. Ward and Donald Brownlee, *Rare Earth: Why Complex Life Is Uncommon in the Universe* (New York: Copernicus Books, 2004), demonstrating the unlikelihood of higher life existing anywhere but on Earth; Charles B. Thaxton, W. L. Bradley, R. L. Olsen, *The Mystery of Life's Origin: Reassessing Current Theories* (New York: Philosophical Library, 1984), arguing that it is highly doubtful that the conditions in the chemical "soup" of primitive Earth can be responsible for the rise of spontaneous life.

8. See Hugh Ross, "Design and the Anthropic Principle," http://www.reasons.org/articles/design-and-the-anthropic-principle; Ross, "Anthropic Principle: A Precise Plan for Humanity, http://www.reasons.org/articles/anthropic-principle-a-precise-plan-for-humanity; and (with reservation) John D. Barrow and Frank J. Tipler, *The Anthropic Cosmological Principle* (Oxford: Oxford, 1988).

9. Hawking and Mlodinow, *Grand Design*, 5.

10. H. Wayne House, "The Law of Causality," *On Intelligent Design*, http://www.hwhouse.com/publications/charts.html; © 2001 H. Wayne House, All rights reserved.

11. Gottfried Wilhelm Leibniz, "Principles of Nature and of

Grace, Founded on Reason," in Leibniz, *The Monadology and Other Philosophical Writings*, trans. with introduction and notes by Robert Latta (Oxford: Clarendon Press, 1898), 415. Leibniz's actual words are, "The first question we are entitled to put will be—*Why does something exist rather than nothing?*" (emphasis added).

12. Ludwig Wittgenstein, *Tractatus Logico-Philosophicus* (New York: Harcourt, Brace & Company, 1922), 6:4312, 184. "The temporal immortality of the soul of man, say, its eternal survival after death is not only guaranteed in any way, but above all do not make this assumption that what you always wanted to achieve with it. But will this solve a mystery that I continue to live forever? Is this eternal life not as enigmatic as the present one? Solving the riddle of life in space and time lies outside space and time." (*"Die zeitliche Unsterblichkeit der Seele des Menschen, das heisst also ihr ewiges Fortleben auch nach dem Tode, ist nicht nur auf keine Weise verbürgt, sondern vor allem leistet diese Annahme gar nicht das, was man immer mit ihr erreichen wollte. Wird denn dadurch ein Rätsel gelöst, dass ich ewig fortlebe? Ist denn dieses ewige Leben dann nicht ebenso rätselhaft wie das gegenwärtige? Die Lösung des Rätsels des Lebens in Raum und Zeit liegt ausserhalb von Raum und Zeit."*)

13. Thomas C. Oden, *The Living God: Systematic Theology* (San Francisco: Harper & Row, 1992), 1:144.

14. Stanley L. Jaki, *Cosmos and Creator* (Edinburgh: Scottish Academic Press, 1981), 71.

15. "How Can You Tell if Something Is Designed? Isn't That Pretty Subjective?" Access Research Network, http://www.arn.org/idfaq/How%20can%20you%20tell%20if%20something%20is%20designed.htm.

16. H. Wayne House, "Specified Complexity Demonstrates Intelligent Design," *On Intelligent Design*, http://www.hwhouse.com/publications/charts.html; © 2001 H. Wayne House. All rights reserved.

17. See Michael Behe, *Darwin's Black Box: The Biochemical Challenge to Evolution* (New York: Free Press, 1996), 39.

18. Charles Darwin, *The Origin of Species: A Facsimile of the First Edition* (Cambridge: Harvard University Press, 1964), 189.

19. Kenneth R. Miller, *Only a Theory* (New York: Viking Penguin, 2008), 54–55.

20. H. Wayne House, "Darwin's Words on What Would Disprove His Theory," *On Intelligent Design*, http://www.hwhouse.com /publications/charts.html; © 2001 H. Wayne House. All rights reserved.

21. C. S. Lewis, *Mere Christianity* (New York: Simon & Schuster, 1996), 25.

22. Hasting Rashdall, *The Theory of Good and Evil* (Chestnut Hill, MA: Adamant Media, 2003), 212.

23. For a discussion of Immanuel Kant and the categorical imperative, see Norman L. Geisler, *Ethics: Alternatives and Issues* (Grand Rapids: Zondervan, 1971), 84–91.

24. Lewis, *Mere Christianity*, 19–21.

25. Pascal, *Pensées* (New York: Dutton , 1958), sec. 3, 68.

26. Norman L. Geisler and Paul Feinberg, *Introduction to Philosophy* (Grand Rapids: Baker, 1987), 268.

27. *Augustini Confessiones* 1.1.1. James J. O'Donnell, Augustine Confessions, vol. 1: Introduction and Text (Oxford: Oxford, 1992), 3. (Latin text by James J. O'Donnell: *"Tu excites ut laudare te delectet, quia fecisti nos ad te et inquietum est cor nostrum donec requiescat in te."*)

28. The answer to question 5 has relied upon material found in H. Wayne House, *Charts on Systematic Theology*, vol. 1, *Prolegomena* (Grand Rapids: Kregel, 2006), 68–71; and H. Wayne House and William Grover, *Does God Feel Your Pain? Finding Answers When Life Hurts* (Eugene, OR: Harvest House, 2009), 108–13.

29. H. Wayne House, "Types of Language That May Be Used

to Speak About God"; © 2003 H. Wayne House. All rights reserved.

30. House and Grover, *Does God Feel Your Pain?*, 110.

Part 2: The Attributes of God

1. Carl F. H. Henry, *God, Revelation and Authority* (Waco, TX: Word, 1976), 4:334.

2. See C. J. Labuschagne, *The Incomparability of Yahweh in the Old Testament* (Leiden, Netherlands: Brill, 1966), 8–20, for further development of these categories.

3. See H. Wayne House and William Grover, *Does God Feel Your Pain? Finding Answers When Life Hurts* (Eugene, OR: Harvest House, 2009), 99–107, for additional discussion on Yahweh's incomparability.

4. Augustus Hopkins Strong, *Systematic Theology* (Philadelphia: American Baptist Publication Society, 1907), 244.

5. W. Robert Cook, *The Christian Faith: Systematic Theology in Outline Form* (Portland: Western Baptist Press, 1981), 108.

6. Gordon H. Clark, "Attributes, the Divine," *Baker's Dictionary of Theology* (Grand Rapids: Baker Book House, 1988), 78.

7. C. C. Ryrie, *A Survey of Bible Doctrine* (Chicago: Moody Press, 1972), 17–18.

8. Strong, *Systematic Theology*, 248.

9. Millard J. Erickson, *Christian Theology* (Grand Rapids: Baker, 1983), 1:299.

10. William G. T. Shedd, *Dogmatic Theology* (Grand Rapids: Zondervan, 1969), 1:338.

11. Louis Berkhof, *Systematic Theology* (Grand Rapids: Eerdmans, 1939), 61.

12. Ibid.

13. Henry C. Thiessen, *Lectures in Systematic Theology*, rev. ed. (Grand Rapids: Eerdmans, 1980), 89.

14. Berkhof, *Systematic Theology*, 60.

15. Thiessen, *Lectures in Systematic Theology*, 78.
16. Ibid.
17. Charles Baker, *A Dispensational Theology* (Grand Rapids: Grace Bible College Publications, 1971), 137.
18. Time should be understood as a measurement of how things relate to each other in a changing world. Since God is changeless in His being and in His sphere of existence above the material world, He cannot be said to be in time. It is not merely that God has endless time or existence, but that He is above it.
19. Berkhof, *Systematic Theology*, 60
20. E. L. Mascall, *The Openness of Being* (London: Westminster Press, 1972), 172.
21. Ronald Barclay Allen, "What Is in a Name?" in William F. Kerr, ed., *God: What Is He Like?* (Carol Stream, IL: Tyndale, 1977), 108–9.
22. For more discussion of these aspects of God's omniscience, see Strong, *Systematic Theology*, 282.
23. Carl F. H. Henry has said that any who argue that God is illogical and then attempt to make an ontological statement about God "indulge in religious babbling." See Henry, *God, Revelation and Authority*, 4:334.
24. For a fuller discussion on the aspect of God's omnipotence, see Millard J. Erickson, *Christian Theology* (Grand Rapids: Baker Books, 1983), 1:276–78.
25. Wayne Grudem, *Systematic Theology: An Introduction to Biblical Doctrine* (Grand Rapids: Zondervan, 1994), 216. We are indebted to Grudem for portions of this section.
26. Erickson, *Christian Theology*, 1:276–77.
27. Grudem, *Systematic Theology*, 216–17.
28. Ibid., 217.
29. Thiessen, *Lectures in Systematic Theology*, 78.
30. Grudem, *Systematic Theology*, 164. The four key words—being, perfections, purposes, and promises—are taken from Berkhof, *Systematic Theology*, 58.

31. Berkhof, *Systematic Theology*, 58.
32. Erickson, *Christian Theology*, 1:278–79.
33. Grudem, *Systematic Theology*, 164–65.
34. Ibid., 164.
35. Erickson, *Christian Theology*, 1:279.
36. For an excellent critique of this movement, see Richard A. Muller, "Incarnation, Immutability and the Case for Classical Theism," *Westminster Theological Journal* 45 (1983): 22–44.
37. Erickson, *Christian Theology*, 1:285.
38. Grudem, *Systematic Theology*, 202.
39. Erickson, *Christian Theology*, 1:284–85.
40. Ibid., 285.
41. Grudem, *Systematic Theology*, 201.
42. Ibid., 197.
43. Ibid.
44. Ibid.
45. Ibid.
46. Erickson, *Christian Theology*, 1:298.
47. Grudem, *Systematic Theology*, 197.
48. Ibid., 198.
49. Ibid.
50. Erickson, *Christian Theology*, 1:294.
51. Ibid.
52. Berkhof, *Systematic Theology*, 76.
53. Ibid., 80.
54. Ibid., 77.
55. Cook, *Christian Faith*, 122.
56. Grudem, *Systematic Theology*, 195.
57. Ibid.
58. Ibid.
59. Ibid.
60. Ibid.
61. Erickson, *Christian Theology*, 1:290.
62. For more on this topic, see H. Wayne House and William

Grover, *Does God Feel Your Pain?* (Eugene, OR: Harvest House, 2009).

63. Cook, *Christian Faith*, 114.
64. Grudem, *Systematic Theology*, 178.
65. Ibid., 177.
66. Erickson, *Christian Theology*, 1:323.
67. Ibid., 1:180.
68. W. Robert Cook, *The Theology of John* (Chicago: Moody Press, 1979), 40.
69. Grudem, *Systematic Theology*, 186.
70. Ibid.
71. Ibid.
72. Ibid. 189–89.
73. Tertullian, for example, a Roman church father of North Africa, was greatly influenced by Stoicism, which in its worst suppositions imagined that God was made up of matter. Even so, as a loyal churchman, Tertullian would never have subscribed to the notion that God was "physical." His pondering whether God was composed of a fine spiritual substance was his way of ensuring God's concrete reality. Tertullian would have become apoplectic had he ever heard about the god of Mormonism, who is very "physical."
74. Erickson, *Christian Theology*, 1:268.
75. Henry, *God, Revelation and Authority*, vol. 6, pt. 2, 302.
76. C. S. Lewis, *Mere Christianity* (New York: Simon & Schuster, 1996), 45.
77. Norman L. Geisler, *If God, Why Evil?* (Minneapolis, MN: Bethany House, 2011), 23.
78. Ibid., 73–78.
79. Ibid., 80–81.

Part 3: The Names of God

1. Carl F. H. Henry, *God, Revelation and Authority* (Waco, TX: Word, 1976), 2:173.

2. Ibid., 180.
3. Louis Berkhof, *Systematic Theology* (Grand Rapids: Eerdmans, 1939), 47.
4. "God, Names of" in Walter A. Elwell, ed., *Baker Encyclopedia of the Bible* (Grand Rapids: Baker, 1988), 1:883. For a full discussion of *Yahweh*, God's proper name, see Henry, *God, Revelation and Authority*, 2:1–25.
5. John H. Walton, Victor H. Matthews, and Mark W. Chavalas, *The IVP Bible Background Commentary: Old Testament* (Downers Grove, IL: InterVarsity Press, 2000), 80.
6. Berkhof, *Systematic Theology*, 47.
7. Henry, *God, Revelation and Authority*, 2:173.
8. On Psalm 2:7, 12, see Allen P. Ross, *A Commentary on the Psalms, 1–41, Kregel Exegetical Library* (Grand Rapids: Kregel, 2011), 207–10 and 212–14, respectively.
9. On the Holy Spirit in the Old Testament, see John F. Walvoord, *The Holy Spirit: A Comprehensive Study of the Person and Work of the Holy Spirit* (Grand Rapids: Zondervan, 1991), 29–54; and Leon J. Wood, *The Holy Spirit in the Old Testament* (Eugene, OR: Wipf and Stock, 1998).
10. In Psalm 82:6 and in Psalm 8:1 some translations render the Hebrew word *elohim* as "God" and others as "angels" or "heavenly beings." See the notes for Psalm 8:5 in the *NET Bible* for a good overview of the translation differences.
11. "Elohim" in Elwell, *Baker Encyclopedia of the Bible*, 1:697.
12. "God, Names of" in Elwell, *Baker Encyclopedia of the Bible*, 1:882.
13. Henry, *God, Revelation and Authority*, 2:171.
14. "God, Names of" in Elwell, *Baker Encyclopedia of the Bible*, 1:885.
15. John Frame, *The Doctrine of God* (Phillipsburg, NJ: P&R, 2002), 349.
16. Ibid., 640.
17. For a fuller list and explanation, see Herman Bavinck, *The*

Doctrine of God, ed. and trans. William Hendriksen (Grand Rapids: Eerdmans, 1951), 86–89.

Part 4: The Trinity and Intrapersonal Relationship of God

1. John Dick, "Lecture XXVIII, On the Trinity," *Lectures on Theology* (New York: Dodd, 1850), 1:286.

2. The Eastern and Western churches differ on this question of the procession of the Holy Spirit, with the Latin church averring that the Spirit proceeds from the Father and the Son (*filioque*), and the Greek church confessing that the Spirit proceeds only from the Father. I have given what I believe is the more tenable view that the Spirit proceeds from the Father eternally, but does so in connection with the Son. Ultimately the Father is the eternal fount of the Son and Spirit.

3. W. Robert Cook, *The Christian Faith: Systematic Theology in Outline Form* (Portland: Western Baptist Press, 1981), 127.

4. See House's article in Dennis W. Jowers and H. Wayne House, *The New Evangelical Subordinationism? Perspectives on the Equality of God the Father and God the Son* (Eugene, OR: Pickwick, 2012), 133–81.

5. The Cappadocian father Gregory of Nazianzus affirms that the reference in John 14:28 does not merely speak of Jesus' humanity when it says that the Father is greater than the Son: "For to say that he is greater than the Son considered as man (τοῦ κατὰ τὸν ἄνθρωπον νοουμένου μείζων), is true indeed, but is no great thing (ἀληθὲς μέν, οὐ μέγα δέ). For what marvel is it if God is greater than man (εἰ μείζων ἀνθρώπου θεός)?" NPNF 2.7.312 (*De filio*) Philip Schaff, *The Nicene and Post-Nicene Fathers Second Series* (Cyril of Jerusalem, Gregory Nazianzen; Oak Harbor: Logos Research Systems, 1997), 2:312.

6. *Orat. c. Ar.* 1:58; Greek and brackets in text added by us. "ἑτερογενὴς ἄρα καὶ ἑτερούσιός ἐστιν ὁ Υἱὸς τῶν γενητῶν, καὶ μᾶλλον τῆς τοῦ Πατρὸς οὐσίας ἴδιος καὶ ὁμοφυὴς τυγχάνει.

Διὰ τοῦτο γὰρ καὶ αὐτὸς ὁ Υἱὸς οὐκ εἴρηκεν, Ὁ Πατήρ μου κρείττων μοῦ ἐστιν, ἵνα μὴ ξένον τις τῆς ἐκείνου φύσεως αὐτὸν ὑπολάβοι· (30) ἀλλὰ μείζων εἶπεν, οὐ μεγέθει τινὶ, οὐδὲ χρόνῳ, ἀλλὰ διὰ τὴν ἐξ αὐτοῦ τοῦ Πατρὸς γέννησιν· πλὴν ὅτι καὶ ἐν τῷ εἰπεῖν, μείζων ἐστὶν, ἔδειξε πάλιν τὴν τῆς οὐσίας ἰδιότητα." Athanasius, *Orationes Tres Contra Arianos.* {TLG 2035.042}; See translation by Archibald Robertson, in NPNF 2.4.340 Athanasius, *Orations Against the Arians* 1.58 (emphasis added).

7. Mark Bird, "Is 'Only-Begottenness' the Proper Basis for the Eternal Submission of the Son to the Father?" (unpublished paper), 11.

Part 5: Early Heresies Relating to God and How the Church Responded to Them

1. For a very readable presentation of heresy in the history of Christianity, see Harold O. J. Brown, *Heresies: The Image of Christ in the Mirror of Heresy and Orthodoxy from the Apostles to the Present* (Garden City, NY: Doubleday, 1984). On monarchianism specifically, see pages 95–103.

2. See Wayne Grudem, *Systematic Theology: An Introduction to Biblical Doctrine* (Grand Rapids: Zondervan, 1994), 241–42.

3. Alister McGrath, *Christian Theology: An Introduction*, 5th ed. (Oxford: Wiley-Blackwell, 2011), 206–7, 245. *Modalism* as a descriptive term for this teaching was introduced into theological vocabulary by the German historian of theology Adolf von Harnack (1851–1930).

4. For an extended discussion, see Brown, *Heresies,* 104–44.

5. Athanasius, "For Discourse Against the Arians I.II," Philip Schaff and Henry Wace, eds., *Nicene and Post-Nicene Fathers,* second series, vol. 4, *St. Athanasius: Select Works and Letters,* 308.

6. McGrath, *Christian Theology,* 275–76.

7. Ibid.

8. Ibid., 277.

9. John Anthony McGuckin, ed. *Ancient Christian Doctrine*, vol. 2, *We Believe in One Lord Jesus Christ* (Downers Grove, IL: InterVarsity Press, 2009), 29–30, 60–61.

10. Grudem, *Systematic Theology*, 243–44.

11. McGuckin, *Ancient Christian Doctrine*, 2:68.

12. Philip Schaff, *The Creeds of Christendom*, 6th ed. (Grand Rapids: Baker, 1983), 1:29.

13. Grudem, *Systematic Theology*, 244.

14. Brown, *Heresies*, 104–105.

15. Ibid., 95–96.

16. Ibid., 96.

17. Ibid., 97.

18. Ibid., 96.

19. Ibid.

20. Clark H. Pinnock, *Most Moved Mover: A Theology of God's Openness* (Grand Rapids: Baker, 2001), 53.

21. David Basinger, "Practical Implications" in Clark Pinnock et al, *The Openness of God* (Downers Grove, IL: InterVarsity Press, 1994), 156.

22. Norman L. Geisler and H. Wayne House, *The Battle for God: Responding to the Challenge of Neotheism* (Grand Rapids: Kregel, 2001), 10–11.

23. Gregory A. Boyd, *God of the Possible* (Grand Rapids: Baker, 2000), 58.

24. Geisler and House, *Battle for God*, 12. For an objective comparison of the views of open theism and classical theology as well as open theism and the doctrine of God through history, see H. Wayne House, *Charts on Open Theism and Orthodoxy* (Grand Rapids: Kregel, 2003).

25. Chart is a revision of one found in Geisler and House, *Battle for God*, 17.

26. For a fuller presentation of these, see Geisler and House, *Battle for God*, 256–88.

27. Ibid., 256.
28. Ibid., 258.
29. Ibid.
30. Ibid., 259.
31. Ibid., 259–60.
32. Pinnock et al., 7.
33. See Geisler and House, *Battle for God*, 275–88.

Part 6: What the Ancient Church Taught About God

1. See the chart "The Gradual Formation of the Apostles' Creed" in Wayne Grudem, *Systematic Theology: An Introduction to Biblical Doctrine* (Grand Rapids: Zondervan, 1994), 583–85. See also Schaff, *The Creeds of Christendom*, vol. 1, *The History of the Creeds*, 14–23.

2. For a very short popular response to this, see Tim Demy and Gary Stewart, *101 Most Puzzling Bible Verses* (Eugene, OR: Harvest House, 2006), 159–60, 195–96. For a thorough study of the issue, see Wayne Grudem, "He Did Not Descend into Hell: A Plea for Following Scripture Instead of the Apostles' Creed," *Journal of the Evangelical Theological Society* 34:1 (March 1991): 103–13. See also Grudem's *Systematic Theology*, 586–94.

3. On the history of each of the early ecumenical councils of Christianity, see Stephen W. Need, *Truly Divine and Truly Human: The Story of Christ and the Seven Ecumenical Councils* (London: SPCK, 2008); and Leo Donald Davis, *The First Seven Ecumenical Councils (325–787): Their History and Theology* (Collegeville, MN: Liturgical, 1983).

4. Arius's letter to Eusebius of Nicomedia, ca. 319, from Theodoret, *Ec. Hist.,* I, IV, *NPNF,* ser. 2, vol. 3, 41.

5. Gerald L. Bray, ed., *Ancient Christian Doctrine*, vol. 2. *We Believe in One God*, Thomas C. Oden, series ed. (Downers Grove, IL: InterVarsity, 2009), ix.

6. See especially John Anthony McGuckin, ed. *Ancient Christian*

Doctrine, vol. 2, *We Believe in One Lord Jesus Christ* (Downers Grove, IL: InterVarsity, 2009–10), 29–73.

7. Allen Ross, "Sound Doctrine: A Study of the Doctrines in the Nicene Creed," http://bible.org/seriespage/god-almighty -maker-heaven-and-earth (accessed September 1, 2012). The entire series is: http://bible.org/seriessound-doctrine-biblical -study-doctrines-nicene-creed.

8. Ibid.

9. See, however, H. Wayne House and Timothy J. Demy, *Answers to Common Questions About Jesus* (Grand Rapids: Kregel, 2011).

10. Jaroslav Pelikan, *Mary Through the Centuries: Her Place in the History of Culture* (New Haven: Yale University Press, 1996), 55.

11. John Anthony McGuckin, "Theotokos," *The Westminster Handbook to Patristic Theology* (Louisville, KY: Westminster, 2004), 330.

12. See Pelikan, *Mary Through the Centuries*, 55–65.

13. "Chalcedon, The Definition of," in F. L. Cross, and E. A. Livingstone, ed., *Oxford Dictionary of the Christian Church*, 3rd ed. (Oxford: Oxford, 1997), 315.

14. Schaff, *The Creeds of Christendom*, vol. 2, The Greek and Latin Creeds, 66.

Part 7: The True and Living God and Other Gods

1. Carl F. H. Henry, *God, Revelation and Authority* (Waco, TX: Word, 1976), 5:10.

2. H. Wayne House and Dennis W. Jowers, *Reasons for Our Hope: An Introduction to Apologetics* (Nashville: B&H, 2010), 358.

3. John Frame, *The Doctrine of God* (Phillipsburg, NJ: P&R, 2002), 347.

4. Todd L. Miles, *A God of Many Understandings? The Gospel and a Theology of Religions* (Nashville: B&H, 2010), 28. See also Harold A. Netland, "Religious Pluralism and the Question

of Truth," in David W. Baker, ed., *Biblical Faith and Other Religions: An Evangelical Assessment* (Grand Rapids: Kregel, 2004), 21–42.

5. See Miles, *A God of Many Understandings*, 33–94.

6. Carl F. H. Henry, *Twilight of a Great Civilization* (Westchester, IL: Crossway, 1988), 59.

7. Norman L. Geisler and H. Wayne House, *The Battle for God: Responding to the Challenge of Neotheism* (Grand Rapids: Kregel, 2001), 303.

8. Carl F. H. Henry, *Remaking the Modern Mind* (Grand Rapids: Eerdmans, 1948), 175. The Archimedian lever (also "Archimdean") refers to the Greek mathematician Archimedes of the third century B.C., who, among other things, studied levers. According to Pappus of Alexandria in his work *Synagogue*, Book 8, Archimedes' work on levers caused him to remark, "Give me a place to stand on and I will move the Earth."

Conclusion

1. Augustine, *Confessions* 1.1.

Recommended Reading

Baker, David W., ed. *Biblical Faith and Other Religions: An Evangelical Assessment.* Grand Rapids: Kregel, 2004.

Bavinck, Herman. *The Doctrine of God.* Edited and translated by William Hendriksen. Grand Rapids: Eerdmans, 1951.

Brown, Harold O. J. *Heresies: The Image of Christ in the Mirror of Heresy and Orthodoxy from the Apostles to the Present.* Garden City, NY: Doubleday, 1984.

Copan, Paul. *Is God a Moral Monster? Making Sense of the Old Testament God.* Grand Rapids: Baker, 2011.

Davis, Leo Donald. *The First Seven Ecumenical Councils (325–787): Their History and Theology.* Collegeville, MN: Liturgical, 1983.

Feinberg, John S. *No One Like Him.* Wheaton, IL: Crossway, 2001.

Frame, John. *The Doctrine of God.* Phillipsburg, NJ: P&R, 2002.

Geisler, Norman L. *If God, Why Evil?* Minneapolis: Bethany House, 2011.

Geisler, Norman L. and H. Wayne House. *The Battle for God: Responding to the Challenge of Neotheism.* Grand Rapids: Kregel, 2001.

Gonzalez, Guillermo and Jay W. Richards. *The Privileged Planet: How Our Place in the Cosmos Is Designed for Discovery.* Washington, DC, Regnery, 2004.

Grudem, Wayne. "He Did Not Descend into Hell: A Plea for Following Scripture Instead of the Apostles' Creed." *Journal of the Evangelical Theological Society* 34:1 (March 1991): 103–13.

———. *Systematic Theology: An Introduction to Biblical Doctrine.* Grand Rapids: Zondervan, 1994.

Hannah, John D. *Our Legacy: The History of Christian Doctrine.* Colorado Springs: NavPress, 2001.

Henry, Carl F. H. *God, Revelation and Authority.* 6 vols. Waco, TX: Word, 1976–83.

———. *Notes on the Doctrine of God.* Boston: W. A. Wilde Co., 1948.

———. *Remaking the Modern Mind.* Grand Rapids: Eerdmans, 1948.

———. *Twilight of a Great Civilization.* Westchester, IL: Crossway, 1988.

House, H. Wayne. *Charts of Christian Theology and Doctrine.* Grand Rapids: Zondervan, 1992.

———. *Charts of World Religions.* Grand Rapids: Zondervan, 2006.

———. *Charts on Open Theism and Orthodoxy.* Grand Rapids: Kregel, 2003.

———. *Charts on Systematic Theology,* Volume 1: Prolegomena. Grand Rapids: Kregel, 2006.

House, H. Wayne and Timothy J. Demy. *Answers to Common Questions About Angels and Demons.* Grand Rapids: Kregel, 2011.

———. *Answers to Common Questions About Jesus.* Grand Rapids: Kregel, 2011.

House, H. Wayne and William Grover. *Does God Feel Your Pain?* Eugene, OR: Harvest House, 2009.

House, H. Wayne and Joseph M. Holden. *Charts of Apologetics and Christian Evidences.* Grand Rapids: Zondervan, 2006.

House, H. Wayne and Dennis W. Jowers. *Reasons for Our Hope: An Introduction to Christian Apologetics.* Nashville: B&H, 2011.

McGrath, Alister E. *Christian Theology: An Introduction,* 5th ed. Oxford: Wiley-Blackwell, 2011.

———. *Dawkins' God: Genes, Memes, and the Meaning of Life.* Hoboken, NJ: Wiley-Blackwell, 2004.

———. *Why God Won't Go Away: Is the New Atheism Running on Empty?* Nashville: Nelson, 2011.

McGrath, Alister E. and Joanna Collicutt McGrath. *The Dawkins Delusion.* Downers Grove, IL: InterVarsity, 2007.

McGuckin, John Anthony. *The Westminster Handbook to Patristic Theology.* Louisville: Westminster, 2004.

Miles, Todd L. *A God of Many Understandings? The Gospel and a Theology of Religions.* Nashville: B&H, 2010.

Motyer, J. A. "The Revelation of the Divine Name." Tyndale Old Testament Lecture, 1959. http://theologicalstudies.org.uk /article_revelation_motyer.html.

Need, Stephen W. *Truly Divine and Truly Human: The Story of Christ and the Seven Ecumenical Councils.* London: SPCK, 2008.

Oden, Thomas C., ed. *Ancient Christian Doctrine.* 5 vols. Downers Grove, IL: InterVarsity, 2009–2010.

Packer, J. I. *Knowing God.* Downers Grove, IL: InterVarsity, 1973.

Pelikan, Jaroslav. *Mary Through the Centuries: Her Place in the History of Culture.* New Haven: Yale University Press, 1996.

Rhodes, Ron. *Why Do Bad Things Happen if God Is Good?* Eugene, OR: Harvest House, 2004.

Ross, Allen P. *A Commentary on the Psalms.* In Kregel Exegetical Commentary, 1:1–41. Grand Rapids: Kregel, 2011.

———. "Sound Doctrine: A Study of the Doctrines in the Nicene Creed." http://bible.org/series/sound-doctrine-biblical -study-doctrines-nicene-creed.

Schaff, Philip, ed. *The Creeds of Christendom, with a History and Critical Notes.* 6th ed., reprint. 3 vols. Grand Rapids: Baker, 2007.

Storms, C. Samuel. *The Grandeur of God.* Grand Rapids, Baker, 1984.

Thaxton, Charles B., Walter L. Bradley, and Roger L. Olsen. *The Mystery of Life's Origin: Reassessing Current Theories.* New York: The Philosophical Library, 1984.

Walvoord, John F. *The Holy Spirit: A Comprehensive Study of the Person and Work of the Holy Spirit.* Grand Rapids: Zondervan, 1991.

Wood, Leon J. *The Holy Spirit in the Old Testament.* Eugene, OR: Wipf and Stock, 1998.

About the Authors

H. Wayne House is Distinguished Research Professor of Theology, Law, and Culture at Faith Evangelical Seminary in Tacoma, Washington, and an adjunct professor of biblical studies and apologetics at Veritas Evangelical Seminary. Formerly he was associate professor of systematic theology at Dallas Theological Seminary; professor of theology and culture at Trinity Graduate School, Trinity International University; and professor of law at Trinity Law School. He has a JD from Regent University School of Law; a ThD from Concordia Seminary, St. Louis; an MA in Patristic Greek from Abilene Christian University; a ThM and MDiv from Western Seminary; and a BA in Classical and Hellenistic Greek from Hardin-Simmons University.

He has been the author, coauthor, and editor of over thirty books, the author of more than seventy journal and magazine publications, and a contributor to several books, dictionaries, and encyclopedias. Among his many books are *The Nelson Study Bible* (NT editor); *The Battle for God*; *Charts on Open Theism and Orthodoxy*; *Charts of World Religions*; *Charts of Christian Theology and Doctrine*; *Chronological and Background Charts of the New Testament*; *Charts of Cults, Sects, and Religious Movements*; *A Christian View of Law*; *Restoring the Constitution*; *The Jesus Who Never Lived*; *Israel: The Land and the People*; *God's Message: Your Sermon*; *Intelligent Design 101*; and *Answers to Common Questions About the Bible*.

Dr. House serves on the board of numerous organizations and

served as president of the Evangelical Theological Society (1991). He leads study tours to Israel every year, and on alternate years to Jordan and Egypt, and Turkey and Greece. He has been married to Leta Frances McConnell for forty-five years and they have two grown children, Carrie and Nathan, and five grandchildren. He may be contacted at info@christianstudytours.com for interest in travel to biblical lands. His website is www.hwhouse.com.

Timothy J. Demy has authored and edited more than two dozen books on the Bible, theology, and current issues. He has also contributed to numerous journals, Bible handbooks, study Bibles, and theological encyclopedias. Among his books are *War, Peace, and Christianity: Questions and Answers from a Just-War Perspective*; *101 Most Puzzling Bible Verses*; *Answers to Common Questions About Angels and Demons*; *Answers to Common Questions About Heaven and Eternity*; *Answers to Common Questions About Jesus*; *Answers to Common Questions about the End Times*; and *Answers to Common Questions About the Bible*. A professor of military ethics at the U.S. Naval War College, he served more than twenty-seven years as a military chaplain in a variety of assignments afloat and ashore with the U.S. Navy, U.S. Marine Corps, and U.S. Coast Guard. He has published and spoken nationally and internationally on issues of war and peace and the role of religion in international relations. He also serves as an adjunct professor of theology at Baptist Bible Seminary in Clarks Summit, Pennsylvania.

In addition to his theological training, which he received at Dallas Theological Seminary (ThM, ThD), he received the MSt in international relations from the University of Cambridge and MA and PhD degrees from Salve Regina University, where he wrote about C. S. Lewis. He also earned graduate degrees in European history and in national security and strategic studies and was the President's Honor Graduate from the U.S. Naval War College. He is a member of numerous professional organizations, including the Evangelical

Theological Society and the Society of Biblical Literature, and is a fellow of the Royal Society of Arts, UK. He and his wife, Lyn, have been married thirty-five years.